POWER PACK ENGLISH

Strategies for using and expanding vocabulary (classes 8–12)

edited by Katharina Einhoff

Linguistic adviser: Josephine Einhoff

Schöningh

Für die Durchsicht des Manuskriptes danken wir sehr herzlich Jürgen Einhoff und Michael Wohlers.

www.schoeningh-schulbuch.de
Schöningh Verlag, Jühenplatz 1–3, 33098 Paderborn

Druck 5 4 3 2 1 / Jahr 2012 11 10 09 08
Die letzte Zahl bezeichnet das Jahr dieses Druckes.

Umschlaggestaltung: INNOVA, Borchen
Illustrationen: Reinhild Kassing, Kassel
Druck und Bindung: westermann druck GmbH, Braunschweig

ISBN 978-3-14-040479-2

Contents

Preface

Welcome to Power Pack English – Strategies for using and expanding vocabulary!

Vocabulary plays an essential role in language learning. Not knowing the words of a language will not allow you to communicate with other people and not knowing the appropriate words will leave you with a feeling of insecurity. Therefore, as a language learner it should be your aim

- to learn a reasonable number of words for the use in both understanding and producing language,
- to memorize words,
- to be able to recall and use your words adequately.

Having acquired a certain amount of words you will, on the whole, understand most of what you hear or read in the foreign language and you will somehow be able to make yourself understood when speaking or writing, but trying to really master a language implies constantly using and expanding your vocabulary, thus making language learning a lifelong process.

Power Pack English – Strategies for using and expanding vocabulary sets out to support you in learning, memorizing and using words of a foreign language successfully. It systematically teaches you a variety of skills and strategies that are important when dealing with vocabulary in a foreign language: You will learn what it really means to know a word. The book provides you with techniques so that you can find out the meaning of unknown words. It introduces you to a variety of different techniques to memorize words. You will find information on how to keep records of words. It tells you what you can do to expand your vocabulary. It contains advice as to what you can do to deal with mistakes. You will learn how to work with a dictionary effectively. It contains a vast variety of motivating games you can play either on your own or with a partner. It features information about what you can do when you cannot come up with the appropriate words.

Every topic is introduced by a **mind map which gives you an overview** of what you will learn in the following chapter. That particular topic is then **explained step by step** and illustrated by **numerous examples**. **Additional tips** are introduced by the symbol "Tip!". The book also contains various **exercises** for you to practise what you have learned already. They are introduced by the symbol "Now over to you". **Solutions** to the exercises can be found in the booklet *Solutions*. The information given on every topic is **summed up in a "Remember" box** at the end of each chapter.

You do not necessarily have to study the whole book. Depending on your personal needs you can choose and work on individual chapters.

In any case, by studying **Power Pack English – Strategies for using and expanding vocabulary** you will become an independent, successful and hopefully motivated learner of the English language.

What do you know?

By answering the following questions find out what you already know about learning and memorizing words.

■ What does it mean "to know a word"?

____

____

____

____

➔ Find more information on how a word is made up on pp. 8 – 24.

■ What do you do when you come across words you do not know?

____

____

____

____

➔ Find more information on how to find out the meaning of an unknown word on pp. 25 – 37.

■ What do you do to memorize words?

____

____

____

____

➔ Find more information on how to memorize words on pp. 38 – 64.

■ How do you store words?

____

____

____

____

➔ Find more information on how you can keep records of words on pp. 65 – 76.

■ What do you do to expand your vocabulary?

➔ Find more information on how to expand your vocabulary on pp. 77 – 80.

■ What do you do with your mistakes?

➔ Find more information on how to deal with mistakes on p. 81 – 82.

■ What kinds of dictionaries are there? What kind of information can you find in a dictionary? When do you consult a dictionary? What do you do to find the information you need?

➔ Find more information on how to work with a dictionary on pp. 83 – 92.

■ What kinds of vocabulary exercises do you like doing?

➔ Find more information on vocabulary games you can play on pp. 93 – 101.

■ What do you do when you want to say something and you are lacking the appropriate words?

➔ Find more information on how to cope with word gaps on pp. 102 – 104.

How a word is made up

A word is made up of a lot of elements.

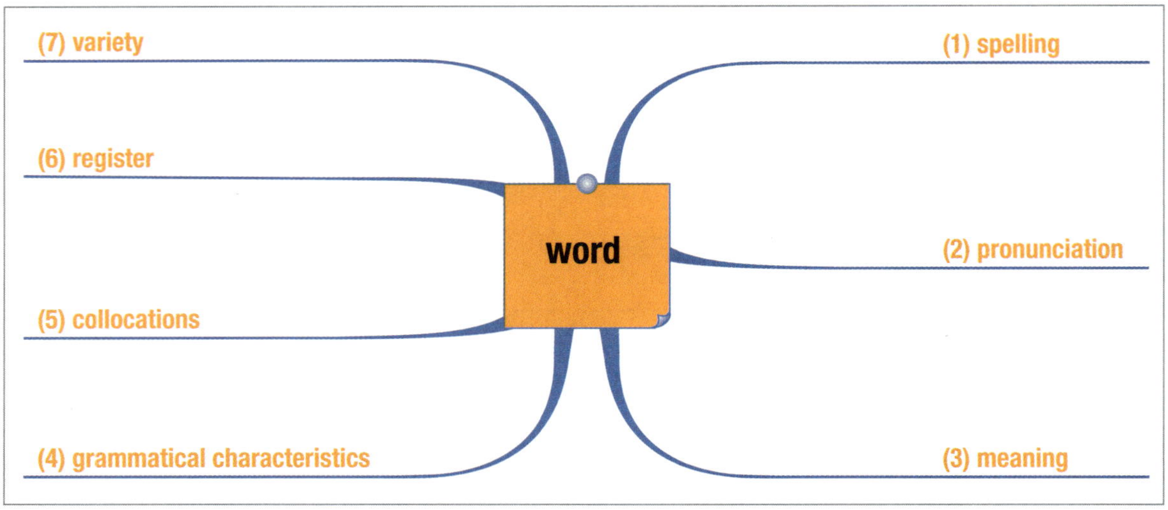

Therefore, really knowing a word implies knowing about all these different elements.

(1) You need to know how a word is spelled

The spelling of a word refers to the way a word is written.

NOW OVER TO YOU

- Cross out some letters and find the hidden words. The words to be found have at least four letters. You don't have to change the order of the letters.

  FGLHJOWDERR ______________________________

  KLBOWVE ______________________________

  MCDOHNMMKLEONTQ ______________________________

  AFDFVMERZTIGHSEDMFENNLT ______________________________

- Find the right order of the jumbled letters.

  g-n-j-t-u-e-d-m-e ______________________

  r-b-a-l-u-y-g-r ______________________

- Fill in the missing letters.

  sp______ch

  coll______gue

  simultan______s

  cons______tious

Sometimes a word is spelled differently, e.g. the following words are spelled differently in British English and in American English:

British English	American English
fav**our**	fav**or**
neighb**our**	neighb**or**
cent**re**	cent**er**
theat**re**	theat**er**
fulfi**l**	fulfi**ll**
enro**l**	enro**ll**
analy**se**	analy**ze**
critici**se**	critici**ze**
lice**nce**	lice**nse**
progra**mme**	progra**m**

Tip! When writing in English you should not mix up British English and American English.

NOW OVER TO YOU

■ Find the corresponding British or American spellings.

British English	American English
colour	
	meter
traveller	
	favorite
	defense
judgement	

(2) You need to know how a word is pronounced

The pronunciation of a word refers to the way a word is spoken. Depending on e.g. the country or the region people come from they pronounce words differently.
In dictionaries you usually find the pronunciation of words in the most common version of British English and sometimes in the most common version of American English. Phonetic symbols tell you how to pronounce a word.

Consonants		Vowels and diphthongs	
b	box	ɑː	car
p	pen	æ	cat
d	door	e	pen
t	ten	ə	about
g	good	ɜː	girl
k	cat	ʌ	cup
f	fish	ɪ	sit
v	very	i	happy
l	leg	iː	people
m	mother	ɒ	song
n	nine	ɔː	fall
ŋ	sing	ʊ	put
r	red	u	February
s	summer	uː	shoe
z	please	aɪ	my
ʃ	she	aʊ	cow
ʒ	television	eɪ	name
tʃ	chocolate	eə	hair
dʒ	jump	ɪə	here
w	wet	oʊ	no
h	he	ɔɪ	boy
j	yes	ʊə	sure
θ	thank you		
ð	this		

Tip! In order to remember what sounds the different phonetic symbols represent try to memorize one easy word for each phonetic symbol.

The symbols / ˈ / and / ˌ / show you how to stress a word.
/ ˈ / shows main stress and / ˌ / shows secondary stress.

Examples: mobile phone / ˌmobile ˈphone/
advertisement /adˈvertisement/

NOW OVER TO YOU

■ Look at the following words. Decide where the main stress is.

honourable
surprise
democracy
refugee
extravagant
to consult
record

How to pronounce the **th** sound

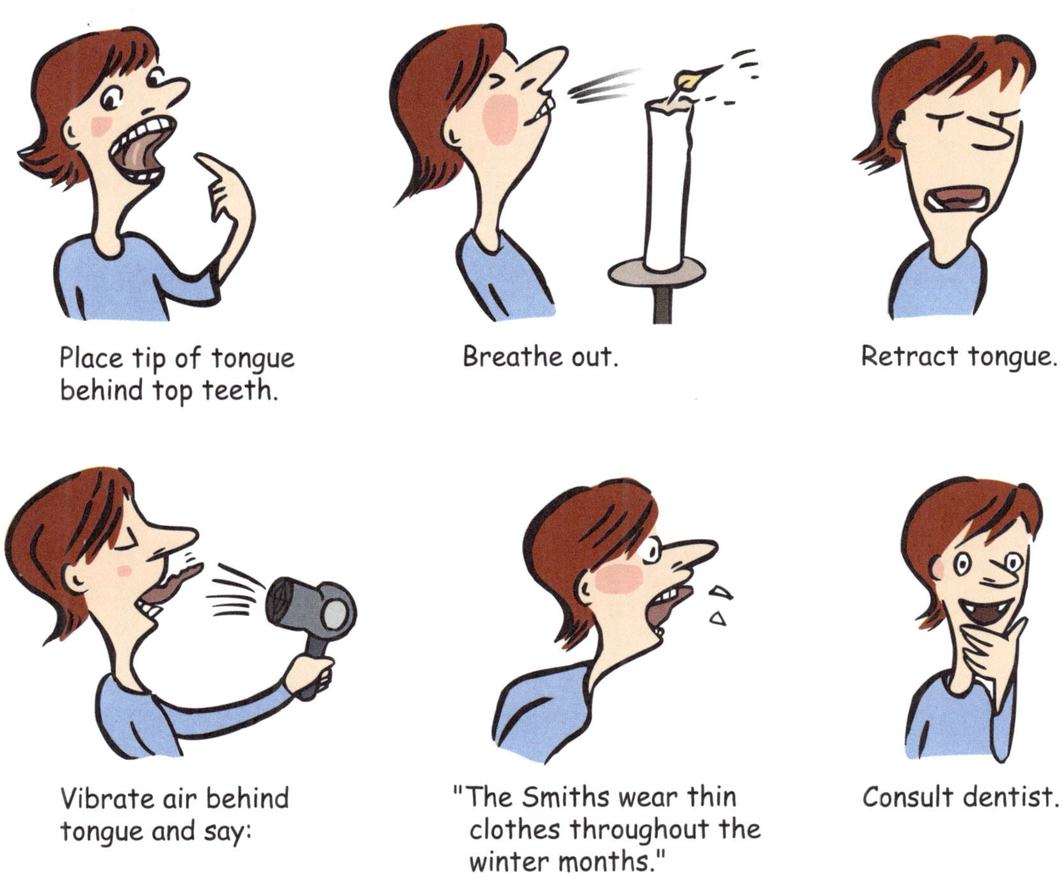

Here are 100 of the most commonly mispronounced words:

abandon
actually
ambiguous
analogous
analysis
anxiety
anxious
architect
associate
auxiliary
awkward
business
candidate
career
catastrophe
characteristic
clothes
colleague
comb
comfortable
comment (noun)/ comment (verb)
committee
colonel
conscientious
contemporary
controversy
cupboard
debt
deliberate
deteriorate
devour
disastrous
effort
electoral
elite
entire
extraordinary
familiar
February
frontier
gauge
grievous
guarantee
harass
height
heir
hiccough
hierarchy
hotel
human
humane
inadequate
indigenous
interesting
interpret
irrelevant
jewellery
lettuce
literary
luxuriant
luxury
maintenance
mankind
melancholic
melancholy
mischievous
monarch
monotonous
mortgage
negotiate
nuclear
numb
opponent
palm
parliament
particular
preface
prejudice
prize
probably
pronunciation
psychiatry
renowned
schedule
semester
severe
spontaneity
subtle
succeed
superiority
supposedly
surface
suspect
sword
tomb
vigorous
wary
weird
worry
yolk

NOW OVER TO YOU

■ Match the sounds and the words.

embarrassed	['dɒktərət]
escape	[kaɪnd]
separate	[ɪm'bærəst]
forward	['sɜːkəmstəns]
kind	['seprət]
unavoidable	[ɪ'skeɪp]
package	['fɔːwəd]
doctorate	['pækɪdʒ]
circumstance	[ˌʌnə'vɔɪdəbl]

■ Find out with the help of a dictionary how the following words are pronounced.

February	appreciate
derogatory	knee
advertisement	efficient
yacht	delicious

Often words share the same spelling, but are pronounced differently. They are called **homographs**.

Examples: We have seats in the back **row**.
They had a terrible **row** about money.

■ How are the following words pronounced? Match them with the corresponding phonetic symbol.

tough	
through	[aʊ]
rough	[oʊ]
dough	[uː]
borough	[ʌ]
cough	[əʊ]
nought	[ɔː]
plough	[ɒ]
enough	
ought	

■ Read out the following sentences. Mind the pronunciation of the words in bold letters.

1. Since there is no time like the **present**, she thought it was time to **present** the **present**.
2. The bandage was **wound** around the **wound**.
3. We have to **wind** up the kite string before the **wind** gets too strong.
4. The soldiers decided to **desert** their **dessert** in the **desert**.
5. There was a big **row** in the first **row** of the cinema.
6. I won't shed a **tear** if you **tear** my old shirt into pieces.

There are as well words that share the same sounds, but are spelled differently. They are called **homophones**.

Examples: What about baking a birthday cake for Tom? All we need is butter, sugar, eggs and **flour** and some baking powder.
He bought me a lovely bunch of **flowers** for my birthday.

■ Choose the right word to fill the gaps.

1. **hear – here**

Come _______________ and sit down next to me.

Did you _______________ the latest news?

2. **knight – night**

A lot of animals hide during the day, but come out at _______________.

It was an honour to be one of King Arthur's _______________.

3. **sea – see**

We are going to spend our holidays near the _______________.

What can you _______________ when looking through the hole?

4. **whether – weather**

What is the _______________ like?

I am not sure _______________ I should ask him if he wants to go with me out tonight.

5. **sight – site**

I cannot see her anymore. She is out of _______________.

Because of the building _______________ there is a traffic jam on the M25.

6. **piece – peace**

They are demonstrating for _______________.

Would you like to have another of _______________ cake?

❼ **break – brake**

Check the ______________ before you go on holiday.

I definitely need ______________ a after this tiring working week.

❽ **stare – stair**

Stop ______________ at me. You are making me nervous.

Mind the ______________.

(3) You need to know what a word means

A word has got one or more meanings, i. e. something it refers to. You can look up the meaning or different meanings of a word in a dictionary.
The word "**tea**" for example refers to the **dried leaves of the tea bush** or to a **hot drink** made by pouring boiling water onto these tea leaves. Some people use the word "tea" either to refer to a **light meal in the afternoon** where sandwiches, cakes and a cup of tea are served or to refer **to a cooked meal served early in the evening**.
Let us have a closer look at the word "tea" used to denote a hot drink. Apart from its main meaning "a hot drink" the word "tea" evokes more ideas and feelings, which are all – in a way – part of the meaning. These ideas and feelings conjured up by a word in addition to its main meaning are called **connotations**. Often these connotations differ depending on the people who use the word. Particularly when people from different cultural backgrounds use a word, misunderstandings can occur because of interculturally different connotations.
Here are possible connotations people in Great Britain have when talking about "tea":

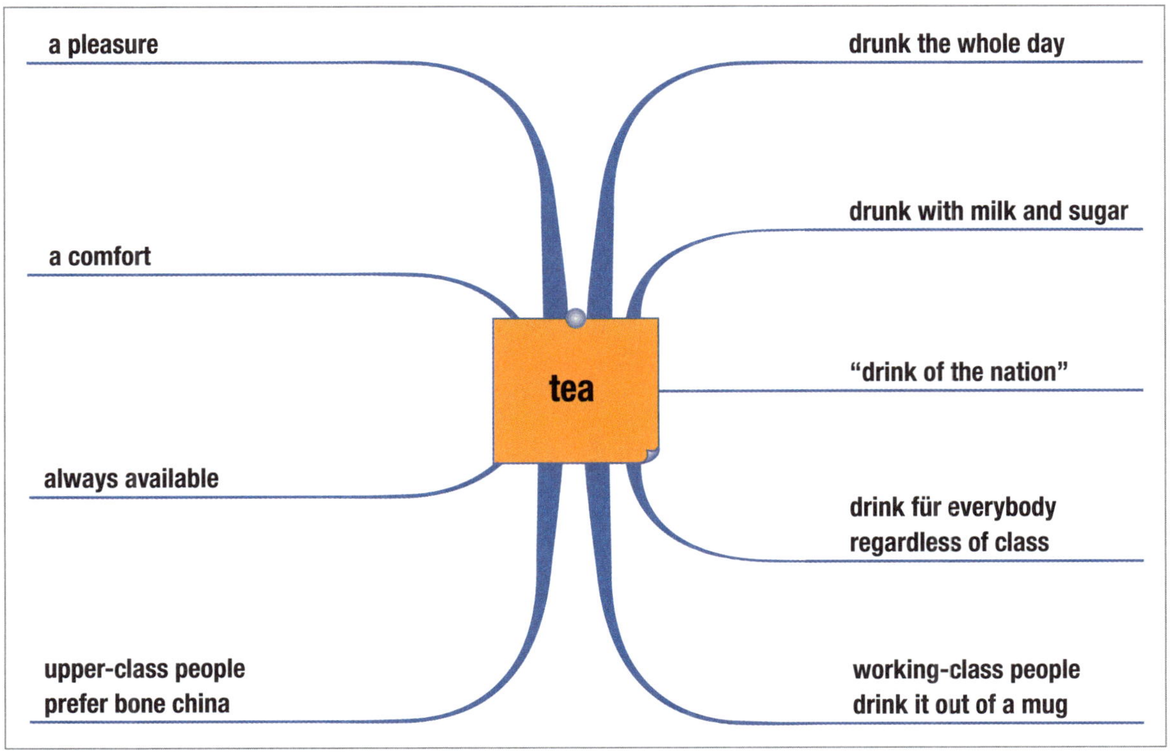

Here are some associations German people have with the word "tea".

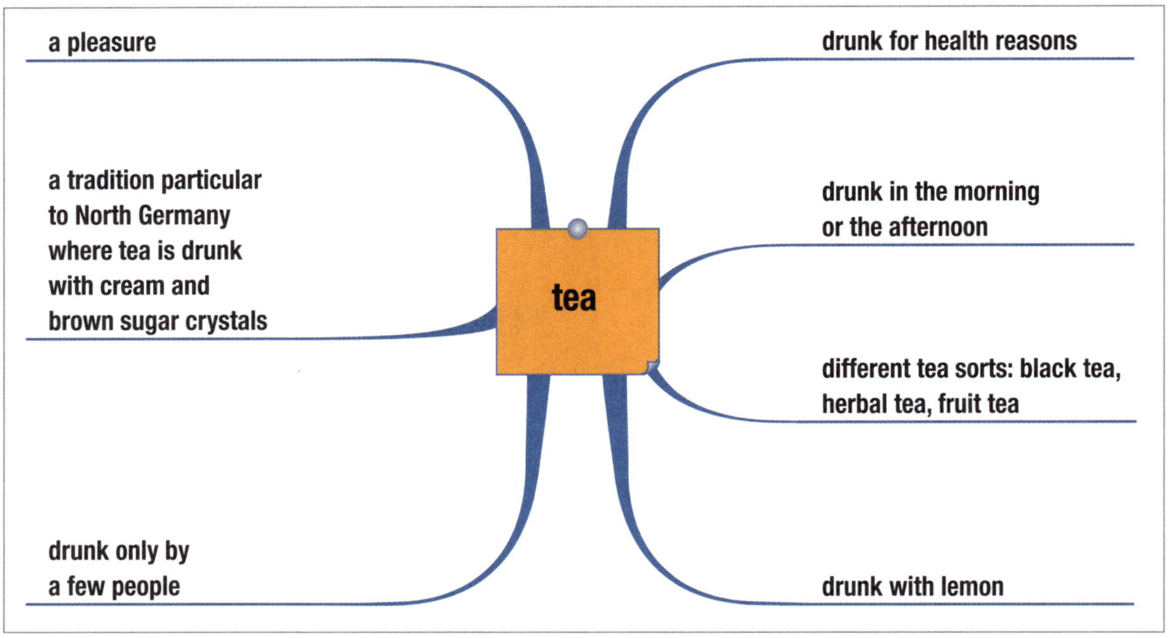

NOW OVER TO YOU

- Find out the meaning of the following words. What connotations do they carry? Try to find out if there are any intercultural differences.

charity rose immigration newspaper

(4) You need to know the grammatical characteristics of a word

Talking about the grammatical characteristics of a word means knowing how to use the word in sentences. Depending on their function in a sentence, words are divided into different word classes.

Example: A crowd of people took to the streets to protest peacefully against the unfair treatment of black students although local authorities had tried to stop them.

Nouns: crowd, people, streets, treatment, students, authorities
Pronouns: them
Verbs: took to, protest, had tried, stop
Adjectives: unfair, black, local
Adverbs: peacefully
Prepositions: of, against
Conjunctions: although
Determiners: a, the

Nouns, verbs, adjectives and adverbs are usually called **content words** as they carry a lot of information whereas pronouns, prepositions, conjunctions and determiners, which contribute to the grammatical structure of a sentence, are called **grammatical words**.

NOW OVER TO YOU

■ Classify the words of the following sentence under the different word classes.

Nowadays blacks still experience a great number of social disadvantages which proves that the civil rights movement never achieved the equality it promised.

Nouns: ______________________________

Pronouns: ______________________________

Verbs: ______________________________

Adjectives: ______________________________

Conjunctions: ______________________________

Determiners: ______________________________

When talking about the individual word classes different grammatical aspects have to be taken into consideration. Here are some examples where grammatical aspects have to be taken into account:

Nouns
- Is the noun countable or uncountable?
- What is the singular, what is the plural form of the noun?

Verbs
- Is the verb an auxiliary verb or a full verb?
- What are the 5 verb forms (the infinitive, the -s form in the 3rd person singular of the present, the -ing form, the simple past form, the past participle)?
- Is the verb regular or irregular?
- What tense is the verb (present tense, present perfect, past tense, past perfect, will-future, going-to future, present progressive, simple present, future progressive, future perfect)?
- What are the passive forms of the verb?
- Is the verb used actively or passively?
- What are the verb complements, i.e. the elements that usually come after a verb (nouns, verbs, adjectives, adverbs, prepositions, etc.)?

Adjectives
- What are the comparative and superlative forms of an adjective?
- What is the position of an adjective in a sentence (before a noun, after certain verbs)?

Adverbs
- What is the form of the adverb?
- What are the comparative and superlative forms of an adverb?
- What is the position of an adverb in a sentence (front-position, mid-position, end-position)?

(5) You need to know the most common collocations of a word

Some words occur together more often than others do, without these words being a fixed unit. These word combinations are called **collocations**. When you learn a word it is helpful to know some collocations of a word. Various combinations are possible, e. g.:

Combination			Example
noun	+	noun	concentration span
noun	+	verb	monarch rule
noun	+	adjective	crystal clear
noun	+	preposition	information about/on
preposition	+	noun	in progress
verb	+	verb	wait and see
verb	+	noun	to commit a crime
verb	+	preposition	to concentrate on
verb	+	adverb	to listen attentively
verb	+	adjective	to drive sb crazy
adjective	+	noun	national identity
adjective	+	preposition	to be keen on
adverb	+	verb	to barely see
adverb	+	adjective	highly controversial

Here are some examples of how words collocate with different words:

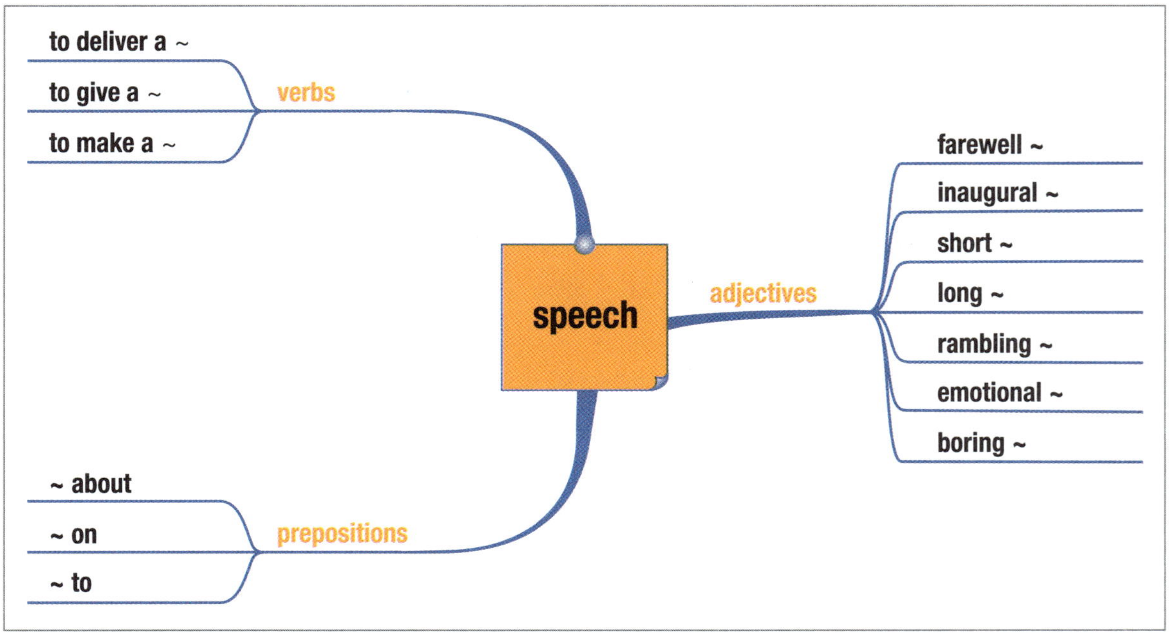

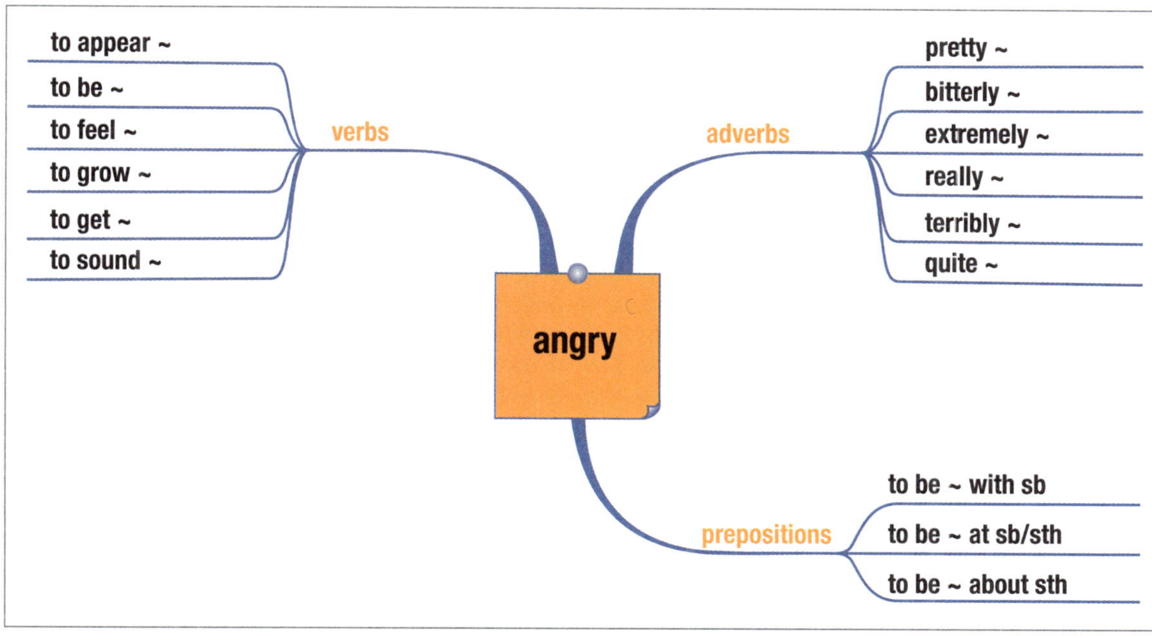

NOW OVER TO YOU

■ Identify and underline as many collocations as possible in the following text.

[…] It all began this time last year, when black students decided that they would begin sharing the shade offered by the tree with their white counterparts, some of whom regarded it as their exclusive preserve.

The next morning three nooses were hanging from the boughs, an image intended to remind blacks of the lynchings once inflicted on their forebears. The white boys found responsible were given three days of in-school suspension after the education chiefs decided that their actions were nothing more than an adolescent prank.

But the incident prompted simmering violence between the two groups, which came to a head during the Thanksgiving holiday last November, when a fire at the school triggered a wave of fights and beatings.

Lawyers representing Mychal Bell, a 17-year-old black student, appealed yesterday to courts to set aside his conviction by an all-white jury over an incident in which a white boy was knocked unconscious. Another five black teenagers were charged with attempted murder relating to the same incident. […]

Civil rights leaders are incensed by the apparent double standards, and are planning a march through the town in support of the "Jena Six" on September 20, when Bell is due to be sentenced. They say that white youths involved in the same cycle of violence faced significantly lesser charges or have been released on probation. […]

Tom Baldwin, The Times, 18.9.2007, p. 37

■ Match the right words to form collocations and form sentences with the collocations you have found.

to have	a trip
to earn	a long time
to break	a match
to take	the flu
to make	a mistake
to gain	experiences
to go on	a page
to win	a meeting
to get	a living
to turn	the news

■ Draw a collocation map for the keyword "opinion".

(6) You need to know the register of a word

Words belong to different registers, i.e. they can be rather **formal**, **neutral** or **informal**. Depending on the situation, you have to choose the appropriate words. Formal words are used in official situations, e.g. in a conversation with your headmaster or when writing an application letter, whereas it is appropriate to use informal words in unofficial or relaxed situations, e.g. when you are talking to members of your family or friends or when you are writing an e-mail to a friend.

Words that are only used by a particular group, e.g. by people working in technical, medical, legal professions or in professions having to do with computers are called **jargon**.

Very informal words which are only used by a particular group, e.g. by teenagers, by musicians or by sports people are called **slang**. Slang words are more common in spoken language. Here are some examples for teenage slang words:

He got **bank** (money).
I **boosted** (stole) these sneakers.
I'm just **chillin** (hanging out without no reason) with my friends.
I'll see you later. **Easy** (Good bye).

As slang words are quickly outdated and often **offensive** you are advised not to use the words yourself.

Furthermore, there are a number of words that are generally considered to be obscene, offensive and shocking. These words are called **taboo words**. They often refer to sex, the body, religion or people's race. You shouldn't use these words.

NOW OVER TO YOU

- Have a look at the following sentences taken from two different letters of complaint, one to a friend and one to a mail-order bookshop. Which sentences are part of the letter to the mail-order bookshop and which sentences are part of the letter to a friend?

I'm just writing to tell you that I feel rather annoyed.
I hope you are ok.
I expect better service from a company of your reputation.
Dear Sir or Madam,
I expect you to replace the damaged books as soon as possible.
Next time I ask you for something, please send it to me straight away, OK?
One of the books has had it.
I am writing to express my dissatisfaction with your mail-order service.
Yours faithfully, ...
I asked you to send me some books I desperately needed for my exams 4 weeks ago.
I was very annoyed at having to wait 4 weeks for the books I had ordered.
What made matters worse was that when they eventually arrived one of the books was damaged in the post.
Take care, ...
On top of all this, I couldn't reach anybody on your hotline.
Hi Mary,
What's more, I couldn't get hold of you on the phone.
So I expect you to buy a new one.
I look forward to hearing from you very soon.

(7) You need to know in which part of the English-speaking world the word is used

English being a world language different varieties of English are spoken all around the world. British people e.g. use different words compared to people from the US or from Australia.
Examples:

British English	American English
advertisement	commercial
aubergine	eggplant
Alsatian	German shepherd
lawyer	attorney
biscuit	cookie
caretaker	janitor
chips	French fries
cupboard	closet
dustbin	garbage can
filling station	gas station
first floor	second floor
football	soccer
holidays	vacation
hoover	vacuum cleaner
injection	shot
letterbox	mailbox
mate	buddy
mobile phone	cell phone
pavement	sidewalk
to queue	to line up
cock	rooster
shop assistant	sales clerk
till	cash register
town centre	downtown
trousers	pants
underground	subway
Wellingtons	rubber boots
zebra crossing	crosswalk

British English	Australian English
excellent	ace
biscuit	bickie
pub	boozer
chocolate	chokkie
farm	station
Go away!	Shove off!
How are you ?	How are you going?
information	oil
New Zealander	kiwi
sausage	snag
sheepfarmer	woolgrower
teacher	chalkie
toilet	comfort station
waterhole	billabong

REMEMBER

Knowing a word involves the following aspects:

You need to know ...

(1) how a word is spelled.
(2) how a word is pronounced.
(3) what a word means (dictionary meanings, connotations).
(4) the grammatical characteristics of a word.
(5) the most common collocations of a word.
(6) the register of a word.
(7) in which part of the English-speaking world the word is used.

Knowing the word "immigration", for example, involves knowing the following aspects of this word:

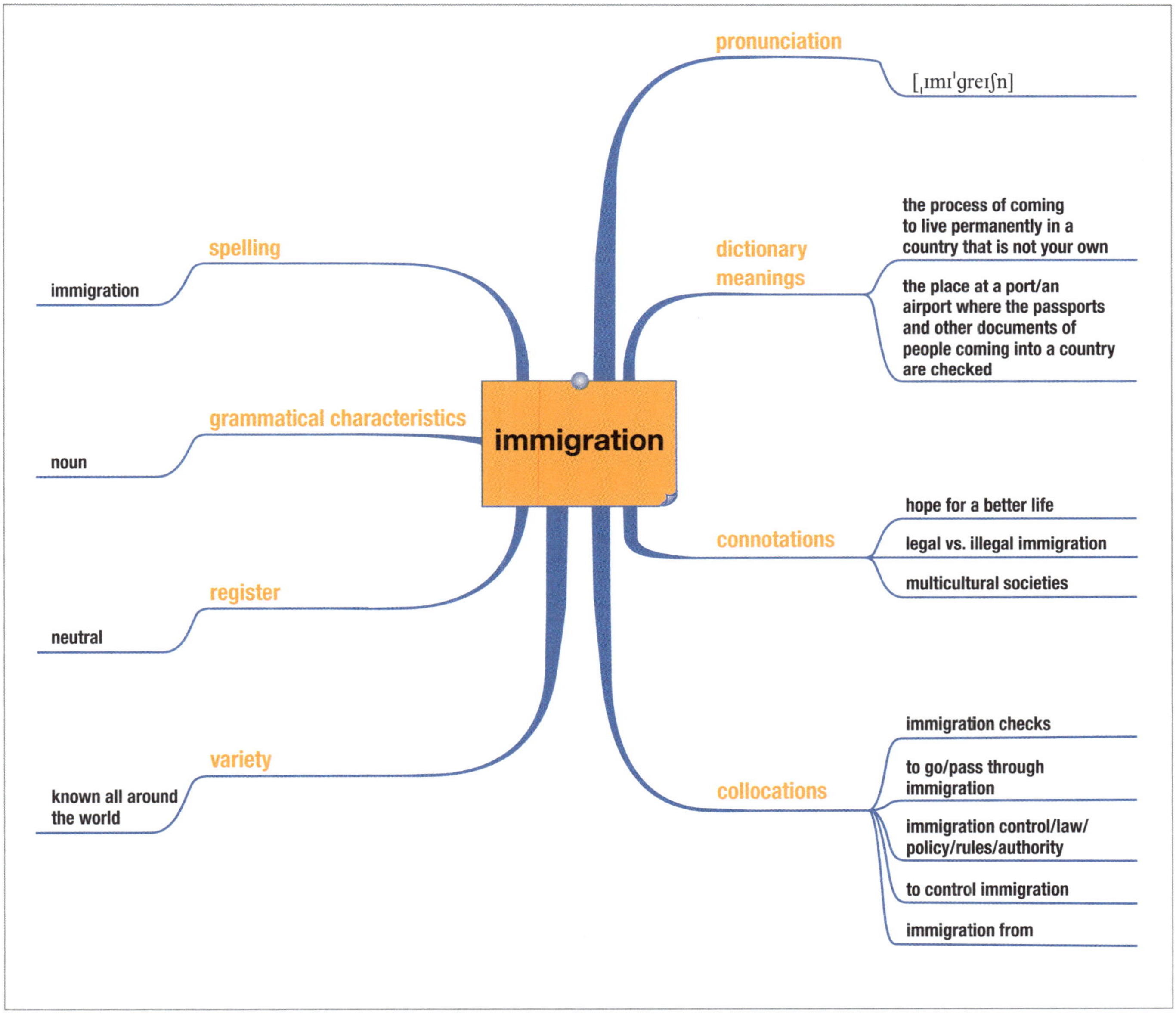

NOW OVER TO YOU

■ Find out with the help of a checklist if you know everything about the following words:

Australia relaxes its immigration rules to persuade skilled young Britons to emigrate.

	to relax	to persuade	immigration rules	skilled
I know how the word is spelled.				
I know how the word is pronounced.				
I know the dictionary meanings of the word.				
I know the word's connotations.				
I know the grammatical characteristics of the word.				
I know the most common collocations of the word.				
I know the register of the word.				
I know in which part of the English-speaking world the word is used.				

Receptive and productive knowledge of words

As you can see knowing a word involves knowing a lot of different aspects. Note that very often you will not know all aspects of a word, e.g. you do not know how it is pronounced as you have only seen it written, but you have not heard it or you are not sure which register a word belongs to.

Apart from differentiating between the different aspects of a word you have to make another distinction when talking about knowing a word: You need to distinguish between the **receptive** and the **productive knowledge** of a word. Receptive knowledge of a word means you understand a word when hearing or reading it, productive knowledge of a word means you know how to use it when speaking or writing it. Sometimes you understand a word when you hear or read it, but you feel uneasy when you want to use it. In this case you have receptive, but not productive knowledge of a word.

We generally understand more words than we use, in other words our receptive knowledge of vocabulary is wider than our productive knowledge.

How to find out the meaning of a word

You are listening to or reading an English text and there are words which you do not understand. First, you should ask yourself if you really need the word to understand the text. **Only if the word seems essential for the understanding of the text**, should you use the following techniques to help you to find out its meaning.

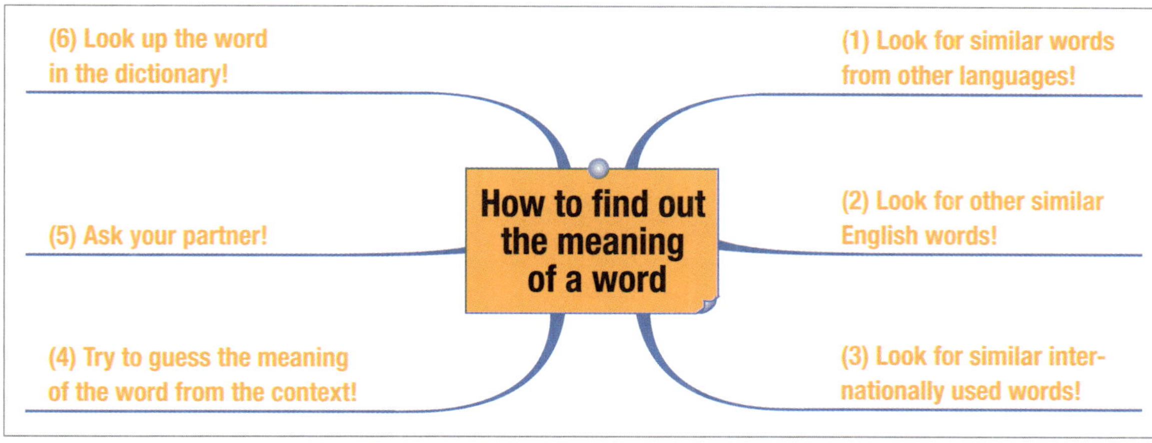

(1) Look for similar words from other languages!

Some English words bear either graphic or acoustic resemblance to their German equivalents or to their equivalents in other languages, e.g. French, Spanish, Italian, Latin.

NOW OVER TO YOU

■ Which German words do the following English words resemble?

English	German
minute	
cathedral	
hand	
fish	
shoe	
brown	
to begin	
disaster	
deficiency	

English words that look or sound like their French equivalents are e.g.

English	French
environment	l'environnement
hospital	l'hôpital
prison	la prison
chamber	la chambre
to resemble	ressembler
envious	envieux/-euse
to enumerate	énumérer
apartment	l'appartement
to announce	annoncer
to contribute	contribuer
to accuse	accuser

NOW OVER TO YOU

- Find other words that resemble German or French words or words from other languages.

Generally, referring to German or to other languages you know, helps you to find the meaning of a word, but there are also words which look similar, but which have different meanings. These words are called "**false friends**". The English word "handy" for example does not have the same meaning as the German word "Handy", which is mobile phone in English, but means "easy to use or do".

Examples:

German word	English equivalent	False friend	German equivalent of false friend
adäquat	suitable, appropriate	adequate	*durchschnittlich*
aktuell	topical, current	actual	*wirklich, tatsächlich*
Annonce	advertisement	announcement	*Ansage, Durchsage*
bekommen	to get	to become	*werden*
brav	well-behaved	brave	*tapfer*
Chips	crisps	chips	*Pommes*
engagiert	committed, involved	engaged	*verlobt, besetzt (Telefon, WC)*
eventuell	possible	eventually	*schließlich*
Gift	poison	gift	*Geschenk*
Gymnasium	grammar school (BE), high school (AE)	gymnasium	*Turnhalle*

German word	English equivalent	False friend	German equivalent of false friend
human	humane	human	*menschlich*
Kollege	colleague	college	*Hochschule*
konsequent	consistent	consequent	*daraus folgend*
Kritik	criticism	critic	*Kritiker*
Meinung	opinion	meaning	*Bedeutung*
mobben	to bully	to mob	*umbringen/ herfallen über*
Note	mark	note	*Notiz*
ordinär	vulgar	ordinary	*gewöhnlich*
Prospekt	brochure, leaflet	prospect	*Aussicht*
realisieren	to put into practice	to realize	*erkennen, sich bewusstmachen*
rentabel	profitable	rentable	*mietbar*
Rente	pension	rent	*Miete*
selbstbewusst	self-confident	self-conscious	*verlegen/unsicher*
sensibel	sensitive	sensible	*vernünftig*
sympathisch	nice	sympathetic	*mitfühlend*
sich wundern	to be surprised	to wonder	*sich fragen*

NOW OVER TO YOU

- Translate the following sentences. Beware of false friends.

1. *Was ist deine Meinung?*

   ____

2. *Sie engagiert sich sehr für den Umweltschutz.*

   ____

3. *Was ist das Thema der heutigen Stunde?*

   ____

4. *Susan hat sich zu einer selbstbewussten Frau entwickelt.*

   ____

5. *Steven ist frustriert, da er seine Idee nicht realisieren kann.*

   ____

6 *In Immobilien zu investieren, ist nicht mehr rentabel.*

7 *Könnte ich dich eventuell am Wochenende sehen?*

8 *Tom wird in der Schule gemobbt.*

(2) Look for other similar English words!

As a result of different word formation rules there are a lot of English words that look similar. Because of these similarities it is often possible for you to work out the meaning of an unknown word by referring to other words you already know in English.

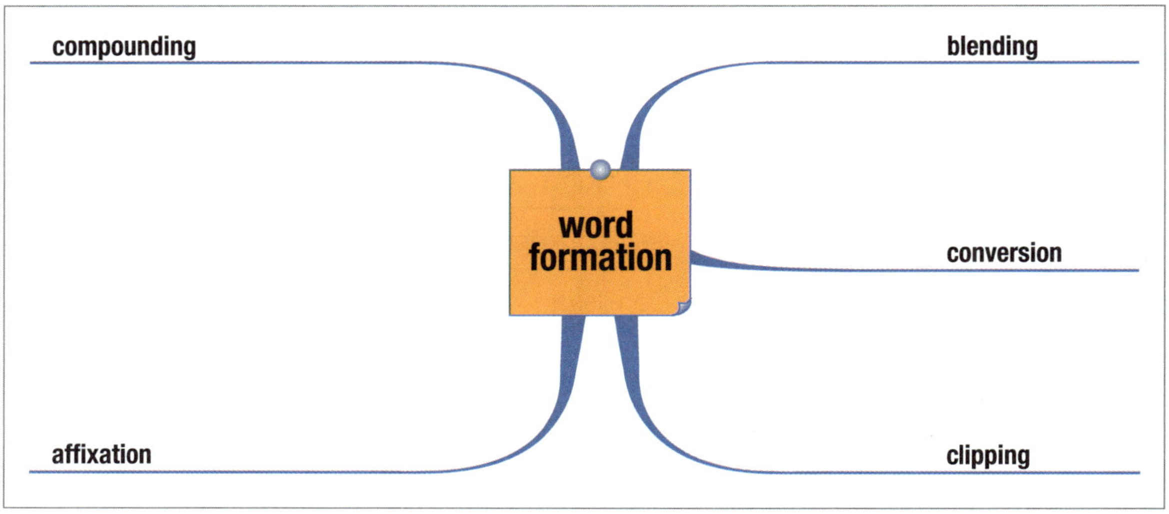

New words are often built by adding a prefix or a suffix to a word stem. This process is called **affixation**. Words that result from adding a prefix or a suffix to a word stem are called **derivatives**.

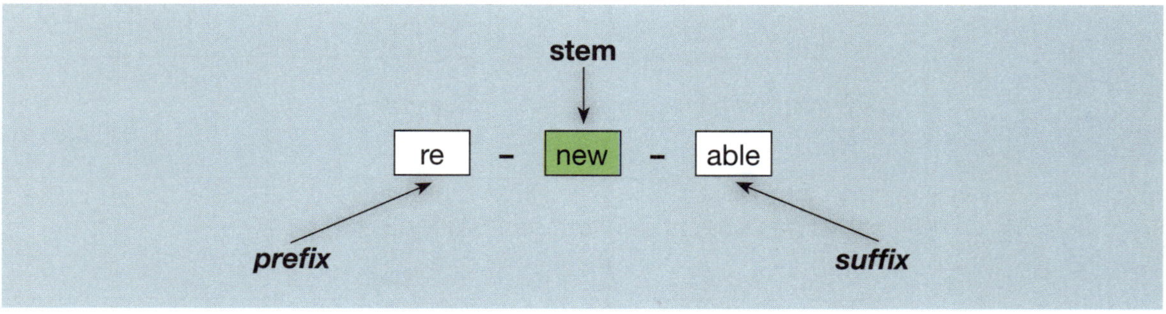

Here are some of the most common prefixes:

Prefix	Meaning	Example
anti-	against	anti-American
bi-	two	bilingual
co-	together	cooperation
counter-	against	counter-productive
de-	opposite of	deforestation
dis-	opposite of	disapproval
ex-	former	ex-president
fore-	before	forename
hyper-	above, over	hyperactive
im-	opposite of	impossible
in-	opposite of	incomparable
inter-	between, among	interactive
ir-	opposite of	irregular
mid-	middle	midnight
mis-	wrong	misunderstanding
multi-	many	multicultural
neo-	new	neoconservative
non-	not	nonsense
post-	later, after	post-war
pre-	before	(to) preoccupy
pro-	in favour of	pro-American
semi-	half	semi-final
sub-	under	subway
re-	again, back	(to) reopen
trans-	across, beyond	transmission
un-	opposite of	unlimited

Here are some of the most common suffixes:

Suffix	Meaning	Example
-able, -ible	which can be done	drinkable, comprehensible
-age	the action or result of	breakage
-al	connected with a process	survival/national
-ance, -ence	the action or state of	confidence
-er	sb who does sth	player
-ful	full of	helpful
-ify	e. g. to make or become	(to) clarify
-ion, -ition, -ation	the action or state of	competition
-ish	e. g. like a	childish
-ism	e. g. the action or result of	criticism, racism
-ize, -ise	e. g. to make or become	(to) realize
-less	without	helpless
-ly	in the way mentioned	happily
-ment	the action or result of	development
-ness	the quality or state of	silliness
-wise	in the manner of	clockwise
-y	e. g. full of	noisy

NOW OVER TO YOU

■ Divide the following words up into their components.

	Prefix	Stem	Suffix
disadvantage			
to rewind			
to simplify			
meaningless			
beautiful			

	Prefix	Stem	Suffix
unbelievable			
indestructible			
unhappiness			

■ Form new words by adding a prefix or a suffix and explain the new meaning of the word.

1. possible ______
2. curious ______
3. treat ______
4. decide ______
5. environment ______
6. beauty ______
7. responsible ______
8. child ______

■ Form as many words as you can from the following prefixes, stems and suffixes.

Prefix	Stem	Suffix
	ject	
	exist	
	agree	
	beauti	
	disciplin	al
inter	hope	ence
re	sider	ary
con	read	ful
ex	happy	ion
pre	na	tion
co	opera	ation
in	struct	ment
dis	harm	er
de	port	able
un	sad	ness
	count	less
	view	
	fer	
	form	
	paint	

Often words are made up of two or more words. These words are called **compounds**. Knowing one or even two or more of the words the compound is made up of helps you to guess the meaning of the compound.

Examples: bedroom, drinking water, telephone box, skyscraper, paperback, second-hand, hairdryer, breathtaking

NOW OVER TO YOU

- Find compounds made up of two nouns by matching words from the boxes below.

arm	path
bed	letter
brain	light
copy	house
day	hole
eye	coat
foot	chair
home	right
key	work
light	storm
mole	shell
news	witness
rain	time
nut	hill

- Find compounds made up of different kinds of words (e.g. nouns, verbs, prepositions) by matching words from the boxes below.

sun	attack
back	ground
counter	developed
down	shine
ghost	long
life	burn
love	sighted
moon	hill
short	sick
under	writer

Sometimes new words are formed by mixing two different words. These new words are called **blends**.

Examples: *brunch* (breakfast + lunch)
infotainment (information + entertainment)
smog (smoke + fog)

Clipping is another word formation process by which longer words are shortenend to one of their parts.

Examples: *ad* (advertisement)
flu (influenza)
exam (examination)
pub (public house)

The process by which words change their word class without changing their form is called **conversion**.

Examples: A trip to the US is an absolute **must**.
Let's **brunch** together tomorrow.

(3) Look for similar internationally used words!

A lot of words are understood in many languages. So it is easy for you to understand the word without having ever heard or read it in an English text.

Examples: definition, philosophy, information, theory, advocate, television, albino, to organize

NOW OVER TO YOU

- Find more international words.

(4) Try to guess the meaning of the word from the context!

The most important source to help you to guess the meaning of a word is the context, i. e. the text itself or additional pictures, cartoons, diagrams, etc., which contain information about the text. In order to guess the meaning of an unknown word have a close look at the words and sentences that come before and after the unknown word. Pay attention to the additional material that accompanies the text as well.

NOW OVER TO YOU

■ Read the following sentences. The words in italics are nonsense words. With the help of the context, i. e. the words that come before and after the nonsense words, try to work out their meaning.

1. I was so *jizzly* that I drank a whole bottle of water.
2. The sun is *jizzling*. Let's go out for a walk.
3. As I didn't work hard enough I *jizzled* all my exams.
4. *Jizzle* from all over the world come to see this stunning exhibition of 20th century art.
5. Can you pass me the *jizzler*. I haven't read today's news yet.
6. When we arrived at the airport we were informed that our *jizzle* had been cancelled.

(5) Ask your partner!

In case you come across an unknown word when talking to someone you can ask him or her to explain the word to you. Here are some phrases for you to ask for an explanation:

– What do you exactly mean by "inalienable"?

– What does "inalienable" stand for?

– Can you explain "inalienable", please?

– Would you mind explaining the meaning of "inalienable"?

– "Inalienable"? Never heard of it.

– I'm not sure if I understood you correctly.

(6) Look the word up in the dictionary!

If none of the above described techniques can help you to find out the meaning of a word you can consult a monolingual or a bilingual dictionary. To get more information how to use a dictionary → pp. 83 – 92.

REMEMBER

Here are the 6 questions you can ask yourself when you do not know a word and you want to find out its meaning:

(1) Do you know any German words or words from other languages which resemble the unknown word?

(2) Do you know any other English words which resemble the unknown word?

(3) Do you know any internationally used words with the same meaning which resemble the unknown word?

(4) Does the context give you any clues as to the meaning of the unknown word?

(5) If you are talking to a person ask him/her to explain the word to you!

(6) Look the word up in a dictionary!

NOW OVER TO YOU

■ Read the following text and decide which technique helped you to find out the meaning of the words underlined. Fill in the table which follows the text.

The Cult of Ethnicity, Good and Bad

A historian argues that multiculturalism threatens the ideal that binds the U.S.

The history of the world has been in great part the history of the mixing of peoples. Modern communication and transport accelerate mass migrations from one continent to another. Ethnic and racial diversity is more than ever a salient fact of the age. But what happens when people of different origins, speaking different languages and professing different religions, inhabit the same locality and live under the same political sovereignty? Ethnic and racial conflict – far more than ideological conflict – is the explosive problem of our times.

On every side today ethnicity is breaking up nations. The Soviet Union, India, Yugoslavia, Ethiopia, are all in crisis. Ethnic tensions disturb and divide Sri Lanka, Burma, Indonesia, Iraq, Cyprus, Nigeria, Angola, Lebanon, Guyana, Trinidad – you name it. Even nations as stable and civilized as Britain and France, Belgium and Spain, face growing ethnic troubles. Is there any large multiethnic state that can be made to work?

The answer to that question has been, until recently, the United States. "No other nation," Margaret Thatcher has said, "has successfully combined people of different races and nations within a single culture." How have Americans succeeded in pulling off this almost unprecedented trick?

Arthur Schlesinger, Time, 8.7.1991, p. 16

I found out the meaning of ...	with the help of German or other languages I know	with the help of English, the target language	with the help of international words
cult	Kult	culture	
multiculturalism			
threaten			
bind			
accelerate			
migration			
continent			
diversity			
salient			
origin			
profess			
inhabit			
locality			
sovereignty			
conflict			
break up			
tension			
disturb			
divide			
stable			
civilized			
face			
trouble			
multiethnic			
successfully			
combine			
pull off			
unprecedented			
trick			

with the help of the context	with the help of a dictionary	Meaning
		Kult

How to memorize words

There are a lot of different techniques to help you to memorize words. Of course, when trying to memorize new words you cannot apply all the techniques at once. You will have to try out the different kinds of techniques and see which ones work best for you.

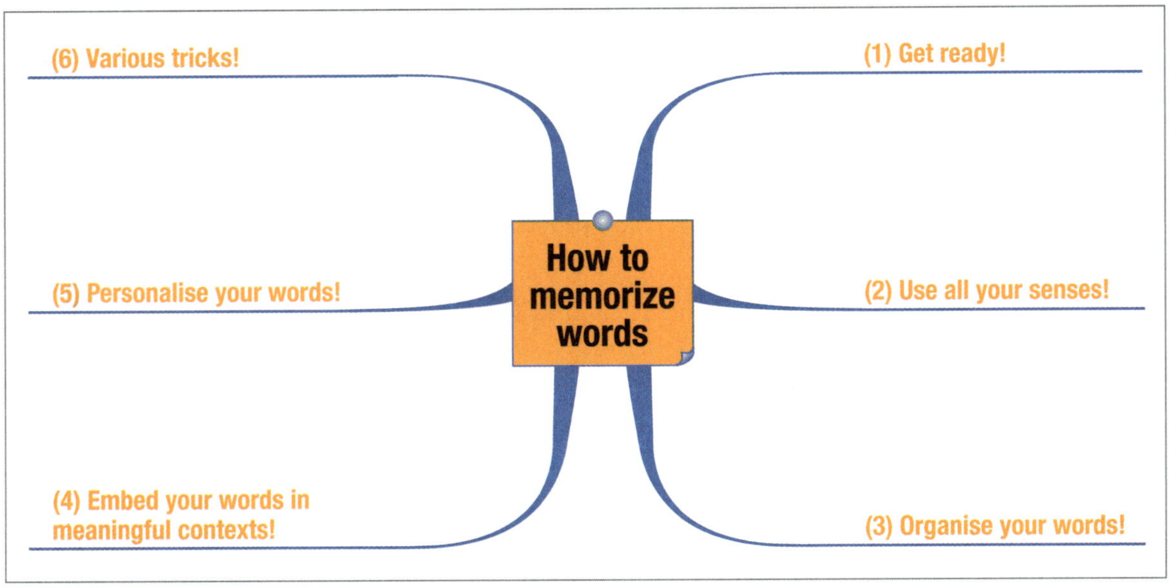

(1) Get ready!

When learning and memorizing new words get in the mood to study. A highly motivated and attentive student will learn and memorize words more easily than an unmotivated and inattentive student.

Concentrate only on your task and avoid anything that could distract you from doing so.

Here are some aspects you should consider when preparing yourself to learn and memorize your words:

- ✓ Tidy up your desk.
- ✓ Air your room.
- ✓ Organise your learning material. Make sure you have got everything you need, e.g. word cards, vocabulary sheets, dictionaries, paper, pens.
- ✓ Make yourself comfortable.
- ✓ Make sure your family and friends don't disturb you.
- ✓ Make sure you switch off the stereo, the radio, the TV or any other source of noise.
- ✓ Don't answer the phone. Postpone all your phone calls to a later time.
- ✓ Give yourself enough time, but set yourself a time limit.
- ✓ …

(2) Use all your senses!

When you learn all your senses are involved. The most commonly known senses are the senses of sight, hearing, smell, taste, touch. Another less recognised sense is the sense of movement.
Depending on the senses that are involved when you learn new words your chances of remembering the words will rise or fall.

Did you know that we remember
10 % of what we **read**?
20 % of what we **hear**?
30 % of what we **see**?
50 % of what we **hear** and **see**?
70 % of what we **write** and **say**?
90 % of what we **do** ourselves?

Of course, every individual learns differently. According to what type of learner they are some people remember words more easily when they **read** them, others need to **hear** the word and others need to **do** something in order to memorize a word.

A learning style questionnaire

Try to find out what learning style you prefer. Read through the following activities. When do you learn and remember most? Tick ✓ the appropriate number of points.

3 points = a lot **2 points = a certain amount** **1 point = a little**

Activity	3	2	1
1. You repeatedly read through a text.			
2. You listen to your teacher giving a talk.			
3. You watch a film.			
4. You repeatedly say aloud the words you need to learn.			
5. You write down the words you need to learn.			
6. You study tables, graphs and charts illustrating the topic you are dealing with.			
7. You like to act out scenes from your course book.			
8. You work with a partner when learning new words.			
9. You like saying tongue-twisters or making up rhymes.			
10. You study any kind of illustration about the topic you are dealing with.			
11. You prefer memorising words by walking around.			
12. Your partner explains something, e.g. a grammar rule to you.			
13. You like giving short talks to your class.			
14. You listen to a recording of the text you are studying.			
15. You try to visualise words in your mind when learning them.			

Count your points. The number of points will show you which learning style you prefer.

Your preferred learning style	Activities	Points
Visual learning style	1 + 3 + 6 + 10 + 15	
Auditory learning style	2 + 4 + 9 + 12 + 14	
Kinaesthetic learning style	5 + 7 + 8 + 11 + 13	

Regardless of the different individual learning styles it is, however, clear that **the more senses are involved when you learn new words, the easier it is to memorize them!** Here are some ideas as to how you can get different senses involved when learning new words:

You can read the word.

Tip! Try to read the word in your mind as well.

You can hear the word.

Tip! You can record the words you want to learn on a tape or on the computer. But make sure you check the pronunciation beforehand. Perhaps your teacher can record them for you. You can then listen to the recorded words and check if you know what they mean or you can check if you know how to spell them by writing them down.

You can write the word.

Tip! Apart from writing them down on a sheet of paper you can, with your finger, "write" the word in the air, on the table, on the floor or on the back of a friend, etc.

You can say the word aloud.

Tip! You can say the word aloud in various ways: Sing it! Shout it! Whisper it! Say it angrily! Say it happily! Say it like a robot would! Say it slowly! Say it quickly! …

If possible, you can actually "study" the real object the word refers to.

Tip! Have a look at the object, if possible listen to the sound it makes, smell it, taste it, touch and feel it.

You can act the word out.

Tip! Ask a partner to learn the words with you by acting them out together. You can also try to invent and play short scenes using the new words.

You can use your imagination …	**to visualize**	**to touch and feel**
	to hear the sound of	**to act out**
	to smell	
	to taste	**… what the word refers to.**

Tip! Relax, close your eyes and concentrate on what you are trying to imagine. Create a picture as vivid as possible in your mind.

You can study a picture of what the word refers to.

Tip! Imagine the picture coming to life.

You can draw a picture illustrating the word.

Tip! Apart from "just" drawing a picture of the word you can e.g. create a **word picture**.

Tip! When drawing a picture of the word you want to learn try to create **a funny or bizarre picture** to enhance the possibility of memorizing it.

to blackmail

mobile phone

a dog-eared book

Tip! When you have to memorize a set of words try to **include them all in a drawing**.

When learning the word BEACH, for example, you can
– read, hear, write and say the word beach,
– visualize a beach in your mind with sand, the sea, waves, shells, seagulls, people, etc.,
– imagine the sound of the waves, the seagulls, the people, etc.,
– imagine the smell of the sea, the wet sand,
– imagine the taste of the salty air,
– imagine what the sand, the water, etc. feels like,
– imagine yourself on the beach,
– have a look at a picture showing a beach,
– draw a picture of a beach,
– act out a scene on the beach.

NOW OVER TO YOU

■ Find out about the meaning of the following words and involve as many senses as possible when memorizing them.

to embrace
mayhem
hedgehog
gentle
fairground

(3) Organise your words!

You can organise the words you want to learn in any way you want. Organising your words seems extremely important in view of the fact that your brain can only process a certain number of items (7+/–2) at a given time, these items being either individual words or word groups forming a unit, called *chunks*. Therefore, the better you organise your words the more effectively you will learn and memorize them.

How can you organise your words?
It is advisable to organise them according to the way they are organised in your mind. Your mind stores words in the **mental lexicon**, a highly organised and interconnected system, in which individual words are stored in various networks according to their form and their meaning.

Here is a choice of the most important principles according to which these networks are organised:

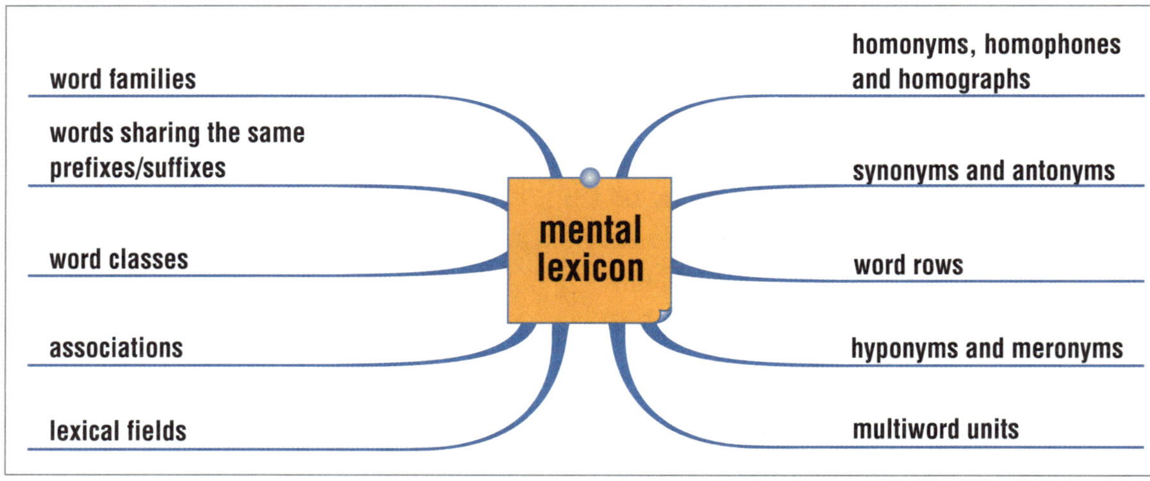

Word classes

You can organise your words according to the word classes they belong to: nouns, pronouns, verbs, adjectives, adverbs, prepositions, conjunctions, determiners (→ pp. 16–17).

Word families

You can organise your words in word families, e.g. words that share the same root, but have different endings.

NOW OVER TO YOU

- Find words (nouns, verbs, adjectives) belonging to the same word family:

to die
aim
satisfaction
to disturb

Words sharing the same prefixes/suffixes

You can organise the words which share the same prefix or the same suffix (➔ pp. 28 – 31).

Homonyms, homophones and homographs

You can organise your words by grouping them together with their homonyms, homophones and homographs.

Homonyms are words that share the same form, but have different meanings.
Example: I like this **book**. (Buch)
I'd like to **book** a holiday to Spain. (buchen)

Homophones are words that share the same sounds, but are spelled differently (➔ p. 14).
Homographs are words that share the same spelling, but are pronounced differently (➔ p. 13).

Synonyms and antonyms

You can organise your words by grouping them together with their synonyms and their antonyms.

Synonyms are words that almost share the same meaning.
Examples: important – essential
false – wrong
incredible - unbelievable
rage – anger

Antonyms are words that have the opposite meaning.
Examples: rich – poor
difficult – easy
to fall – to rise
different – similar

NOW OVER TO YOU

■ Find synonyms and antonyms for the following words.

	Synonyms	Antonyms
to deteriorate		
exciting		
to loathe		
miserable		

illegal		
disdain		
furious		
heat		
to pursue		
bias		
important		

Word rows

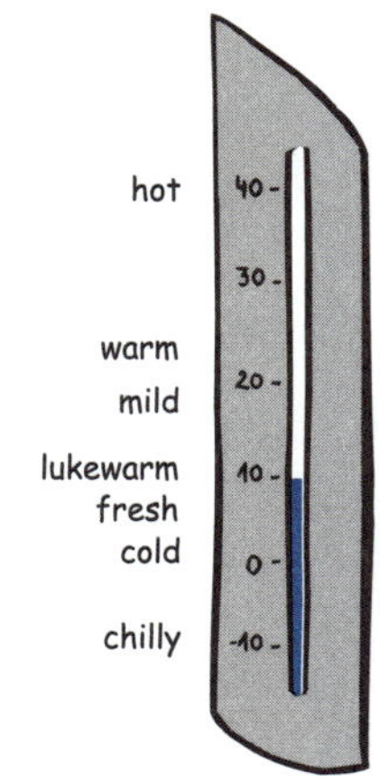

You can organise your words in word rows. There are different kinds of word rows.

Word rows can be organised, for example, according to **differences between words**.

to stroll   to walk   to march   to run   to rush

Furthermore, word rows can express the **chronological order** of different actions, called action chains, e. g.: What are the usual events in a person's life?

to go to school   to leave home   to study   to have children   to graduate   to find a job   to retire

NOW OVER TO YOU

- Organise the following words and expressions in word rows.

1. obese – bony – thin – chubby – skinny – fat – slim
2. to hate – to like – to love – to loathe – to adore – to dislike
3. to enjoy your holiday – to pay the bill – to arrive at the hotel – to book a room – to check-out – to return home – to register at the reception
4. to go to the platform – to get on the train – to get off the train – to find a seat – to store the luggage – to buy a ticket – to go to the station

- Find words and expressions to create word rows starting as follows:

tiny – ______________________________

birth – ______________________________

to study a recipe for a cake – ______________________________

____

Hyponyms and meronyms

You can organise your words by grouping them together with their hyponyms or meronyms.

Hyponyms are words whose meaning is included in a more general word. They express a "a kind of"-relationship. *A cat – a dog – a horse – a bird* for example are hyponyms of *animal*. The words *a cat – a dog – a horse – a bird* ranking at the same level are called **co-hyponyms**, the word *animal* being the **superordinate** term.

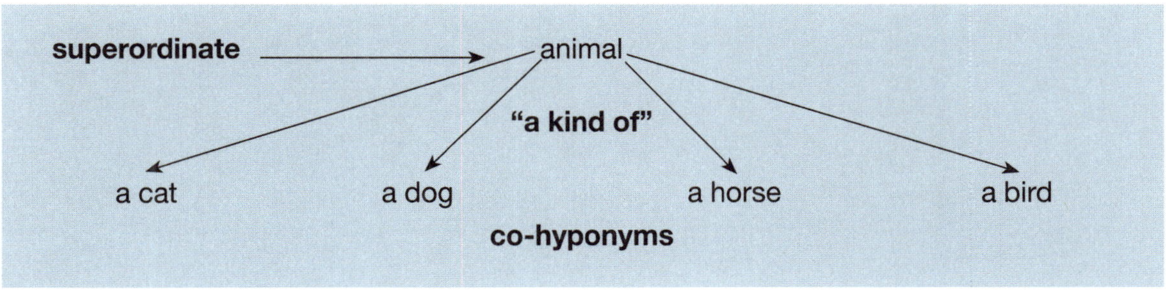

Words that have a "a part of "-relationship are called **meronyms**. *Hand* is a meronym of body, or *room* is a meronym of *house*, for example.

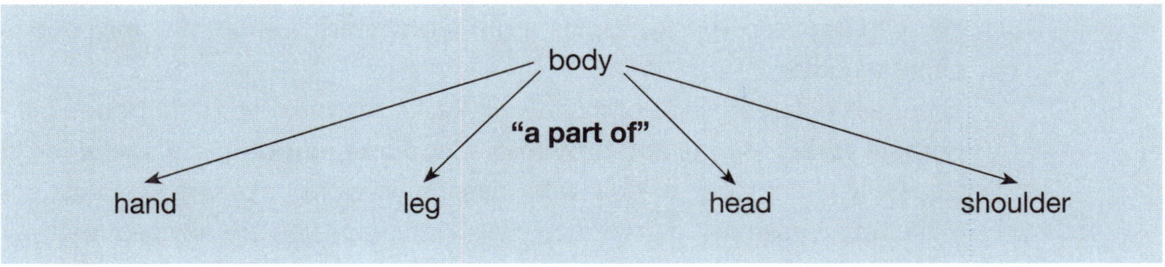

NOW OVER TO YOU

■ Find hyponyms for the words "furniture" and "fruit".

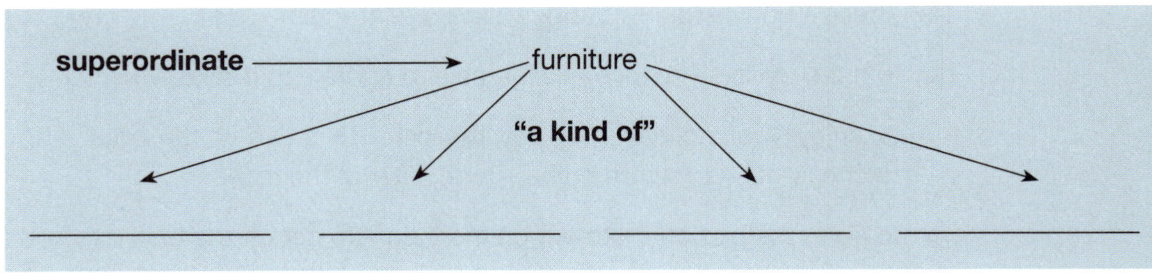

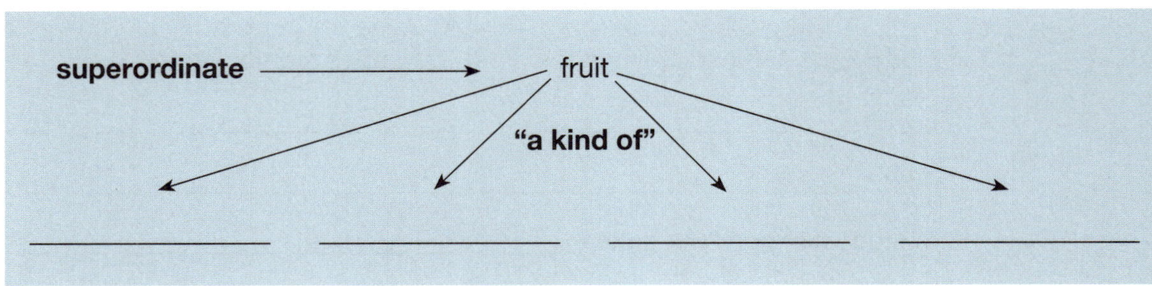

■ Find meronyms for the words "school" and "house".

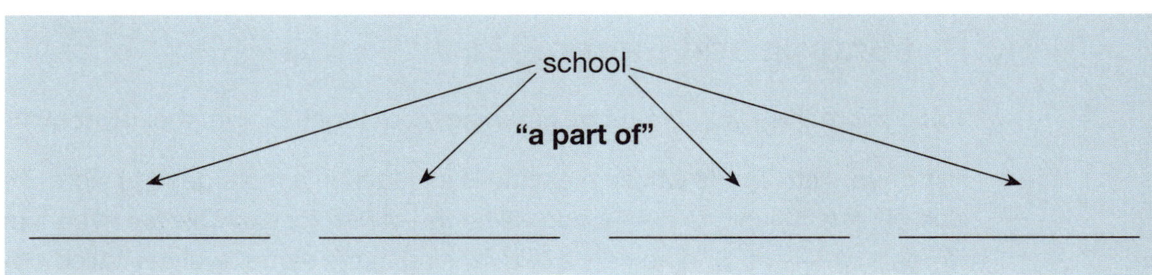

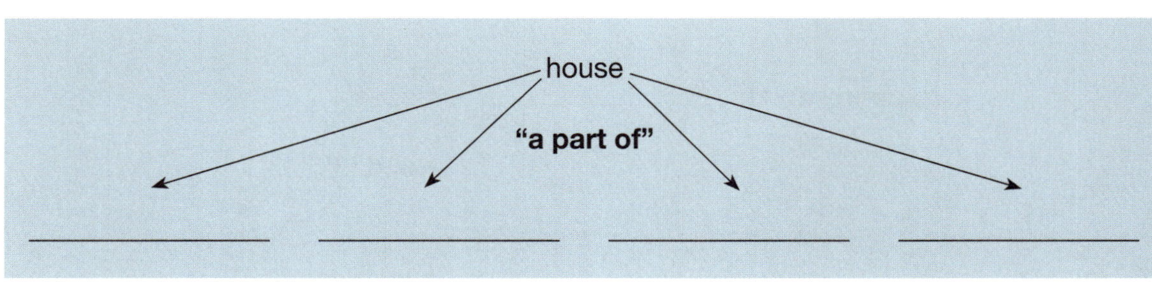

Multi-word units

You can organise your words as **multi-word units**, i.e. word combinations that very often occur together.
There are different kinds of multi-word units, the most important ones being **collocations, phrasal verbs, idioms and proverbs, discourse markers and social formulae**.
Generally it is difficult to deal with these multi-word units in a systematic way. But as they make up an essential part of the English language you are advised to always learn them as what they are – as units. If possible, they should always be learned within a short context.

Tip! When reading an English text try to identify as many multi-word units as possible. Underline them and copy them into your vocabulary book or onto word cards. Make sure that you write down whole sentences. Underline the new phrases. Look up their meanings in a dictionary. Then write your own sentences with the newly learned phrases.

a) Collocations

For a definition of what a collocation is, examples and exercises → p. 18.

b) Phrasal verbs

Phrasal verbs are verbs that are followed by a so-called particle, which can be a preposition (e.g. to get up) or an adverb (e.g. to fall asleep). Some verbs are even followed by 2 particles (e.g. to put up with). The particle or particles following the verb can change the whole meaning of a verb.

Phrasal verbs are usually used in informal spoken and written English (e.g. to **put off** a meeting) whereas other verbs derived from Latin are preferred in formal written English (e.g. to **postpone** a meeting). Phrasal verbs are grouped as follows:

Intransitive verbs: They don't take an object.
Example: The headmaster asked the pupils who had witnessed the fight to <u>come forward</u>.

Transitive verbs: They can take an object.
- **Inseparable verbs:** The object must always come after the particle.
  Example: The teacher is always <u>getting at</u> **me**.
- **Separable verbs:** The object can either come between the verb and the particle or after the verb. If the object is a pronoun it must come between the verb and the particle.
  Example: <u>Put</u> **that book** <u>down</u>. It doesn't belong to you.
  <u>Put</u> **it** <u>down</u>.

Here are some useful phrasal verbs:

to make	
to make for sth	to head for sth
to make sb/sth into	to change sb/sth
to make off	to leave in a hurry
to make sth out	to be just able to see or hear sth
to make sb out	to understand sb's character
to make sth up	to pretend that sth is true to deceive sb
to make up for sth	to compensate for sth
to do	
to do away with sb (*inf*)	to kill sb
to do away with sth (*inf*)	to get rid of sth/to abolish sth
to do sth up	to fasten a coat, skirt, etc. to renovate an old building or to repair a car, etc. to decorate sth in a particular way

to do with sb/sth	to need or to want sb/sth
to do without sb/sth	to manage without sb/sth
to bring	
to bring sth about	to make sth happen
to bring sth back	to return sth
to bring sb down	to remove from power to make sb fall
to bring sth down	to reduce sth to land an aircraft to make an animal fall out of the sky by shooting it
to bring sth forward	to move sth to an earlier time to suggest sth for discussion
to bring sth out	to produce sth/to publish sth
to bring sb (a)round	to make sb become conscious again to persuade sb to agree to sth to bring sb to sb's house
to bring sb together	to arrange for people to meet and do sth together to make people end a disagreement
to bring sb up	to raise a child
to bring sth up	to mention a subject or start a talk about to vomit
to come	
to come across sb/sth	to find sb/sth by chance/to meet
to come along	to go to a place with sb
to come apart	to fall into pieces
to come back	to return
to come between	to separate
to come down with sth	to get an illness
to come forward	to offer help
to come out	to be published
to come out with sth	to say sth unusual or unexpected
to come round	to visit sb
to come up	to be mentioned (e.g. an idea)
to come up against sb/sth	to have to deal with difficulties with sb/sth

to go	
to go after sb/sth	to follow sb/sth
to go ahead with sth	to start to do sth
to go along with sb/sth	to agree with sb/sth
to go away	to leave a place or person
to go off	to leave to explode to make a noise
to go on	to continue to happen
to go out with sb	to have a relationship with sb
to go over sth	to think very carefully about sth/to examine sth
to go through sth	to experience a difficult situation to search sth to read or discuss sth
to go up	to increase
to get	
to get sth across	to communicate sth successfully
to get along	to have a friendly relationship
to get at sb	to criticise sb
to get away	to escape
to get away with sth	to do sth wrong without being punished
to get back	to return
to get behind	to fail to do sth at the right time
to get by	to manage
to get down to sth	to start sth difficult
to get on	to have a friendly relationship
to get out of sth	to avoid a responsibility
to get over sth	to recover from an illness
to get through sth	to do an amount of work to come to a successful end
to get together	to meet
to get up	to get out of bed

to put	
to put sth across	to explain sth to sb
to put sth away	to tidy up
to put sb down	to criticise/to belittle sb
to put sth forward	to suggest sth
to put sb off	to discourage
to put sth off	to delay to postpone to cancel
to put sth on	to present (e.g. a concert, a play) to dress
to put sth out	to extinguish to switch off
to put sb up	to give accommodation
to put up with sth	to tolerate sth without complaining
to set	
to set about sth	to start doing sth
to set sb/sth apart	to make sb/sth different from other people
to set sth back	to delay sth
to set off	to begin a journey
to set sth off	to make sth happen
to set out	to begin sth with a particular aim in mind
to set sth up	to establish sth
to take	
to be taken aback	to be very surprised at/about sth
to take after sb	to resemble sb
to take sb/sth away	to remove sb/sth
to take sth back	to withdraw sth
to take sth in	to understand sth
to take off	to leave the ground
to take sb on	to employ sb
to take to sb/sth	to start to like sb/sth
to take sth up	to start sth

to look	
to look after sb/sth	to take care of sb/sth
to look ahead	to think about the future
to look back	to think about the past
to look down on sb	to think that you are better than sb
to look for sb/sth	to try to find sb/sth
to look forward to sth	to be excited about sth in the future
to look into sth	to investigate
to look sth up	to try to find information (e.g. in a book)

NOW OVER TO YOU

■ Match the following phrasal verbs with their synonym.

to get back	to be disappointed
to let down	to arrive
to come round	to come to an end
to turn up	to investigate
to break down	to accompany sb about to set off on a journey
to run out of	to return
to look into	to recover consciousness
to see someone off	to stop working

■ Identify and underline the phrasal verbs in the following sentences and explain their meaning.

1. We are planning to do up our living-room next autumn.
2. Can you make out the woman standing next to the church?
3. We've got enough room to put you up for the weekend.
4. You'll have to do without your hat. I forgot it at home.
5. What do you make of our new English teacher?
6. Tom always gets away with his lies.
7. They were born in India, but they were brought up in the U.S.
8. The airline's superb service made up for all the inconveniences caused by the delay of our flight.
9. Susan always comes up with good ideas.
10. We'll have to take on more staff to be able to finish the project in time.

⓫ The theatre is putting on *Macbeth* next year.

⓬ Our children really get on well.

⓭ She went on doing sports till her eighties.

⓮ He took to her at first sight.

⓯ I'm not putting up with your bad mood anymore.

c) Idioms

Idioms are fixed multi-word units whose meaning is different from the dictionary meanings of the individual words. They are very hard to understand and learn.

NOW OVER TO YOU

■ Match the following idioms with the corresponding expression.

He's fallen **head over heels** in love with her.	to try
When she left she **broke my heart**.	a nuisance/a difficult person
It's raining. That's why she has **got the blues** today.	very underweight
Climbing up that tree is not very difficult. Why not **have a go**?	to be miserable
We didn't book a flight in advance. We thought we'd just go to the airport and **take pot luck**.	to cause despair to another
She hasn't eaten much lately. She is all **skin and bones**.	to go/leave
It's late. I think we should **make a move**.	to correct an unfair situation
I really regret what I have done. I will have to **right a wrong**.	to earn a lot of money quickly and easily
She seems to have a good job. She is **coining money**.	completely and thoughtlessly
Stop bothering me. You are **a pain in the neck**.	to leave things to chance
To put it in a nutshell, this discussion is a waste of time.	to be very scared
Coming face to face with the bear, I felt **scared stiff**.	to say it in a few words

d) Proverbs

As **proverbs** are highly idiomatic expressions they are very difficult to understand and to learn.

NOW OVER TO YOU

■ Match the following proverbs with the corresponding paraphrases.

Don't count your chickens before they're hatched.	If something is not planned it will never take place.
Barking dogs seldom bite.	A friend who helps when you are in trouble is a true friend.
Any time means no time.	Someone speaks frankly and directly.
Too many cooks spoil the broth.	Don't make plans for the future too early.
Call a spade a spade.	Rumours are usually based on some truth.
A friend in need is a good friend indeed.	You have to choose between two equally bad alternatives.
Between the devil and the deep blue sea.	Those who loudly threat to do something rarely do so.
There is no smoke without fire.	Things will go wrong if too many people interfere.

e) Discourse markers

Discourse markers are words or short expressions that organise what we are saying and writing.

Common discourse markers used in **spoken everyday English** are e.g.

- **Now**, what shall we do next?
- **Well**, where shall we go?
- **Hang on!** I need to get my umbrella.
- **Let me see**, I'm sure I left it in the car.

Discourse markers used in **discussions** are e.g.

- What I'm really interested in is …/What I'd like to know …
- I suggest that we …/Why don't we …
- Let me explain to you …/Let me put it in other words./What I'm trying to get at …
- I'm afraid, I …/Sorry, but …/I don't know if …/Would you mind if …
- In my opinion, …/Personally speaking, I think …/If I were you I'd …/If you ask me …
- I agree with sb about/on …/I disagree with sb about/on …

Common discourse markers **in written English** to help you organise **a comment** are e.g.

- The problem/topic I am going to deal with is …/In the following text, I am going to deal with …
- There have been heated discussions about …
- In my opinion …/To my mind …/I think …/I take the view that …
- To begin with …/In the first place …/The first point to mention is …
- I would like to give examples …/… for example/for instance …

- … in other words …
- On the one hand … on the other hand …
- I would like to refer to …/With regard to the fact that …
- It is also important …/Furthermore …
- Lastly, …/But the most important point is …
- As a result …/To sum up the arguments …/Summing up, we can say …/In conclusion …/ To cut a long story short …/We can draw the conclusion that …

f) Social formulae

Social formulae help you to get along in everyday situations. Social formulae are e.g.

- How are you? I'm fine.
- What's up? What's new?
- I'd better get going.
- See you later./Have a nice day.
- Nice to meet you./Pleased to meet you.
- Let's get together some time.
- Sit down and make yourself at home.
- Please help yourself.
- Thank you. You're welcome.
- I'd like you to meet …

NOW OVER TO YOU

■ Imagine situations in which you would use the social formulae mentioned above.

Lexical fields

You can organise your words in **lexical fields**. A lexical field contains words that have some kind of thematic relationship. Lexical fields could be e.g.

Education in Great Britain/the U.S.
The economy
Migration
Urban life
The media
Politics in Great Britain/the U.S.
Terrorism
The world of work
…
The environment
Technology and progress

Associations

You can organise your words into **association networks**. An association network contains words that **only you** associate with a given keyword.

Tip! When you make an association network you should include all kinds of word classes, i.e. nouns, verbs, adjectives, etc.

For information as to how to create an association network → p. 69.

(4) Embed your words in meaningful contexts!

Try out the following experiment:

- Have a look at the 20 individual words below and try to memorize them during the next 5 minutes:

  permission – mobile phone – to travel – nephew – recently – handkerchief – imaginary – to laugh – exhausted – to hide – innocent – witness – noise – ugly – to interrupt – to allow – opinion – to convince – obviously

- Note down as many words as you can remember.
- Now use the 20 words to create a story as vividly as possible during the next 5 minutes.
- How many words are you able to remember this time?
- You will have found it easier to remember the words and you will have probably remembered more words than before.

This is because your brain can memorize words more easily when they are embedded in some kind of meaningful context. Here are some possibilities for you to create meaningful contexts when memorizing new words:

- Form your own sentences containing the new words.
- Write a story using the new words.
- Find or invent a joke, a rhyme, a poem, etc. containing the new words.

Tip! The funnier or crazier your sentences, stories, quotations, jokes, rhymes, poems, etc. are, the better!

(5) Personalise your words!

When trying to memorize new words it is important to get personally involved. The more the words mean to you personally, the higher the chances that you will memorize them. If, for example, your parents or grandparents have immigrated to the country you are living in, you will find it easier to learn words having to do with the topic of immigration.
Of course, not all the words that you want or have to learn necessarily contain personally relevant meanings. But nevertheless you can try and find some. Here are some ideas for you to personalize words:

- Create sentences about yourself, your family or your friends incorporating the new words.
- Create your own jokes, rhymes, poems or stories using the new words.
- Create association networks (→ p. 69).
- Rank the new words as to your personal preference. Explain your ranking.
  Do you like the sound and look of a word or do you rather like the meaning of the word?

NOW OVER TO YOU

■ In order to memorize the following words try to personalize them.

approval – current – brief – petrified – overwhelmed – disappointment – to be made redundant – flee from – to be in charge of – to enable – as a matter of fact – attempt

(6) Various tricks!

Here are some more methods of memorizing new words effectively.

The method of loci

The method of loci, having been practised since classical times, is a well-known and widely acknowledged technique in order to memorize items. You imagine a familiar place, e.g. your house/flat, your room, your school or a familiar route you regularly take, e.g. the route you take to go to school or the route you take to go to the next supermarket. Then you mentally put the words you want to memorize somewhere around the place or somewhere along the route. In order to remember the words you take an imaginary walk around the room or along the route, recalling all the words you have "placed" there.

Alternative: Instead of just imagining where you would "place" the words you can actually write them down on post-its and stick them to different places in your room or house or flat. You will automatically learn the words *en passant*. You can recall them by mentally walking around your room or house or flat.

The finger method

Associate each word you want to memorize with a finger. This method, of course, is only suitable if you only want to learn a small number of words.

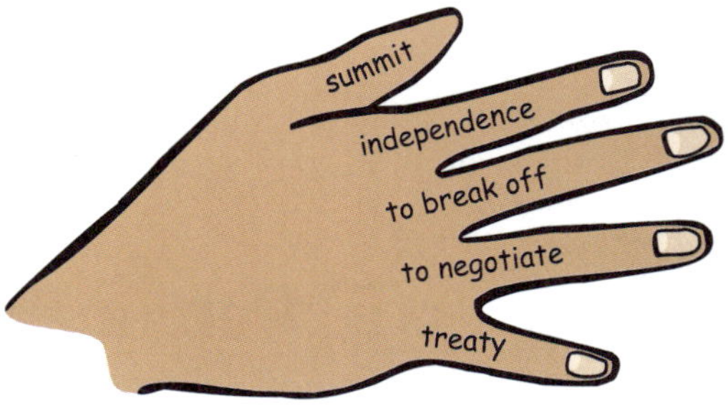

"A landscape of words"

To learn the words referring to items around you, you can write down the names of these items on post-its and stick them onto the real things, thereby creating a "landscape of words". Look up the items you do not know in English in a dictionary. As the words you have found will mostly be nouns try to find appropriate verbs, adverbs, adjectives, etc. to go with these nouns and write them down on the post-its as well.

The learning poster

Write down on a large sheet of paper (DIN A3) the words you want to learn, illustrating them if you want to. When finished pin the poster to the wall. You will learn the words *en passant*.

Acronyms/Acrostics

Acronyms and Acrostics are another helpful way of memorizing words. **Acronyms** are a kind of abbreviations. They are formed by only using the first letters of words, e.g. AIDS being an acronym for "acquired immune deficiency syndrome", NATO for "North Atlantic Treaty Organisation" or FBI for "Federal Bureau of Investigation".
Acrostics are poems or other pieces of writing, in which the first letter, syllable or word of each line can be read downwards to form a word or expression.

Example: **T** ECHNIQUE
E NERGY
C ONTROVERSIAL
H UMAN
N UCLEAR POWER
O UT OF CONTROL
L ABORATORY
O RGAN
G ENETIC ENGINEERING
Y OU

NOW OVER TO YOU

- Create an acrostic from the following word: GENETIC ENGINEERING. Try to find words which have to do with the topic "genetic engineering". Write a short text integrating all the words you have found.

The keyword method

The keyword method helps you to recall new words.

– Establish an acoustic and visual link between the new word and a known German or English word.
– Combine the word you want to learn and the word you know in a mental image.

Example: You want to learn the English expression *to give someone the sack*. First find a keyword for the word to learn. Sack sounds and looks like the German word *Sack*. The German word *Sack* will serve as the keyword. Then link these two words visually by imagining a picture of the two items, e.g. a person being carried out of the manager's office in a sack.

NOW OVER TO YOU

- Using the keyword method memorize the following words: to apply for a job. Draw a picture.

(7) Revise your words!

Unfortunately, over time we tend to forget what we have learned. The German psychologist Hermann Ebbinghaus (1850–1909) illustrated this phenomenon in the so-called *forgetting curve*, which shows at what rate we forget newly learned material. According to this curve we forget new information at the following rate:

After 20 minutes	about 40 %
After 1 hour	over 50 %
After a day	over 60 %
After a week	over 70 %
After a month	over 80 %

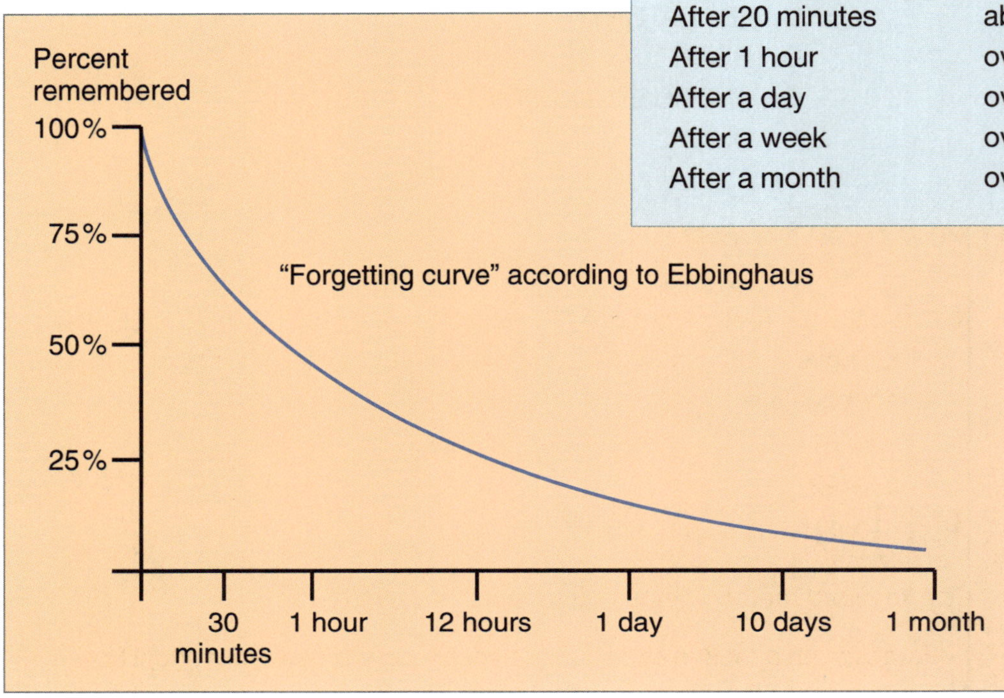

Ebbinghaus's "forgetting curve" is based on learning meaningless material. When learning meaningful material the amount and speed of memory loss is likely to be reduced, but is still significant. One of the ways to successfully stop this process of forgetting is to regularly revise what you have learned.
Effective learning and revision of words and expressions involves taking into consideration the following aspects:

- **How many** words do you want to learn or revise at a time?
- **When** do you learn or revise your words?
- **How much time** do you spend on learning or revising words?
- **How often** do you learn or revise the newly learned words?
- **How** do you learn or revise your words (with the help of your English book, of your own vocabulary list or of word cards/by reading or writing or saying the words aloud/…)?

But first of all, in order to find out about how you learn or revise your words fill in the following table:

	Which words did you learn/revise?	How many words did you learn/revise?	When did you learn/revise your words?	How much time did you spend on learning/revising your words?	How did you learn/revise your words?
Monday, the …					
Tuesday, the …					
Wednesday, the …					
Thursday, the …					
Friday, the …					
Saturday, the …					
Sunday, the …					

Here are some **mistakes** which are often made:

- You learn or revise too many words at a time.
- You spend too much time on a set of words.
- You prefer learning and revising your words all at once rather than spreading out your learning and revising over a period of time.
- If you spread your learning and revising out you either do not allow enough time between your sessions or else you allow too much time.
- You always learn or revise your words in the same way.

Instead, you should go by the following rules when learning:

Rules for revision

- As your brain can only memorize a limited number of individual items (**as a rule 7 +/–2**) do not learn or revise more than this amount of words at a time.
- Spend at least **1 minute on each word**.
- Do not spend more than **10–15 minutes per learning session**.
- **Space out the time** you want to spend on learning or revising a set of words rather than massing it together in a single block. Ideally you revise your words according to the following schedule:

Learn the new words.

1st	revision after a couple of hours
2nd	revision after a day
3rd	revision after a week*
4th	revision after a month
5th	revision after half a year

* If you think a week is too long to wait for the 3rd revision you can already revise the words and expressions earlier.

- Most learners require **5–7 revisions** in order to learn a set of words. As soon as you are sure that you know a word do not revise it anymore. You risk “overlearning” it.
- **Give yourself time** to learn or revise your words (e.g. on the school bus, during a free period, while waiting in a queue, shortly before or after doing your homework, before going out with friends, before having your evening meal, before going to bed).
- **Do not learn or revise the words of two languages** one after the other. You risk mixing them up.
- **Do not watch TV or play on the computer** immediately after you have learned or revised your words. When confronted with a flood of new stimuli coming from the TV pictures or the computer you risk forgetting what you have just learned.
- **Vary the way you learn or revise words**. This book gives you a lot of ideas of how to learn words in a creative way.
- **Make the learning and revision of words a daily routine**.

NOW OVER TO YOU

■ For the words you want to learn next week set up a schedule as the one on p. 63. Keep in mind the rules mentioned above.

	Which words do you want to learn/ revise?	How many words do you want to learn/ revise?	When do you want to learn/revise your words?	How much time do you want to spend on learning/revising your words?	How do you want to learn/revise your words?
Monday, the …					
Tuesday, the …					
Wednesday, the …					
Thursday, the …					
Friday, the …					
Saturday, the …					
Sunday, the …					

(8) Use them or lose them!

Using your newly learned words is the best way to make sure that you will eventually know them. Ideally, you should use the new words in real-life situations. Therefore, seek out as many opportunities for real-life practice as you can. Otherwise, there are different exercises to use the new words. P. 93 offers a variety of exercises on that purpose.

REMEMBER

The more you "work" with the words you want to learn the higher the chances that you will know them in the long run!

Remember what you can do to memorize words and expressions:

(1) Get ready!
Be motivated and attentive.

(2) Use all your senses!
Involve as many senses as possible when learning and memorizing words.

(3) Organise your words!
Choose among the various ways of organising your words the most appropriate one.

(4) Embed your words in meaningful contexts!
Create a suitable meaningful context for the words you want to learn and memorize.

(5) Personalize your words!
Make words mean something to you.

(6) Various tricks!
Make use of different mnemonic devices such as the method of loci, the finger method, the learning landscape, the learning poster, acronyms/acrostics, the keyword method to learn and memorize words.

(7) Revise your words!
Carefully time your revision and make sure you vary the way you revise your words.

(8) Use them or lose them!
Practise your words by using them as often as possible, e. g. in different exercises.

How to keep records of words

There are various techniques to store words, all having advantages and disadvantages. These are the three most applied techniques:

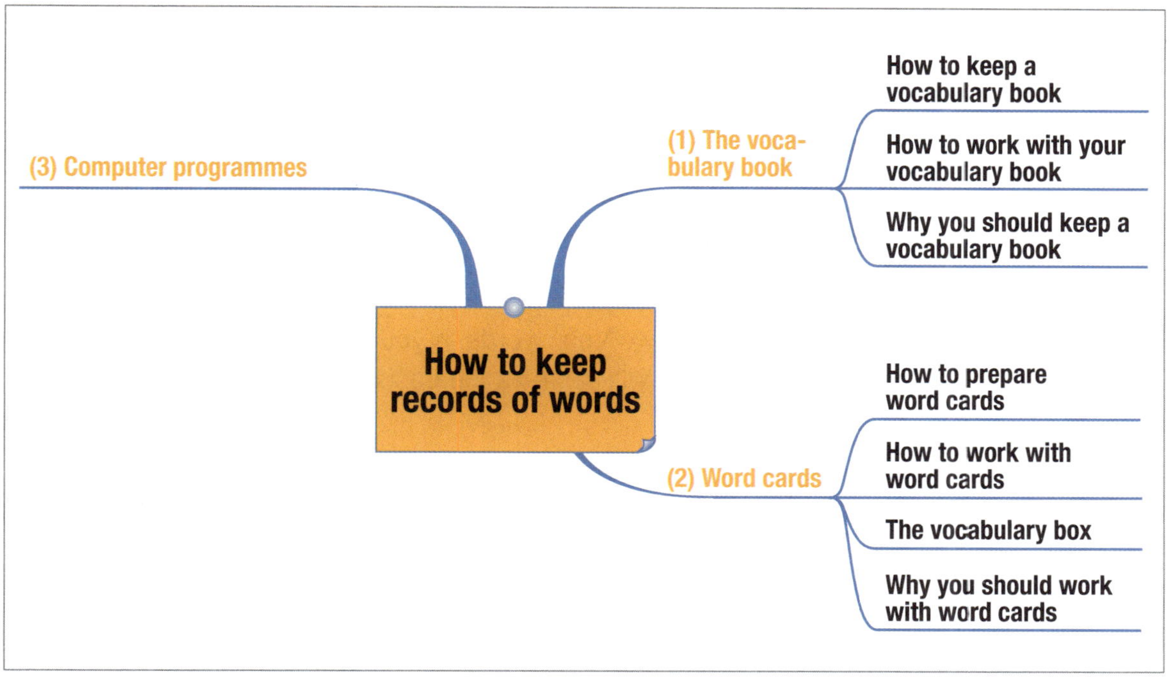

When deciding on how to store words, keep in mind what you expect from your record:
- You want to revise sets of related words, not individual words.
- You want to find the word easily when you need it.
- You want to test yourself.
- You want to add information to individual words.
- You want to add words to the words you have already recorded.

(1) The vocabulary book

A vocabulary book represents a systematic way of storing words. All you need is a DIN A4 folder with several file sheets to which more sheets can be added at any time.

How to keep a vocabulary book

When keeping a vocabulary book it is important that you **organise your words**. Remember the different **organising principles** (➔ pp. 43 – 56). You can e. g.
- collect words of the same word family,
- gather words sharing the same prefix/suffix,
- find synonyms and antonyms,
- write down word rows,
- note down as many collocations as possible for the individual words,
- write down phrasal verbs with their different meanings,
- gather idioms,

– collect proverbs,
– write down discourse markers for different purposes, e.g. to be able to take part in a discussion or to write a comment,
– gather words that belong to the same lexical field,
– make a list of words that you associate with a keyword,
– group together false friends,
– note down your favourite words and expressions,
– list your problem words,
– …

Having decided on how to organise your words you can
– write them down in **systematic word lists** or
– make use of different **visualizing techniques** to note them down.

Tip! When writing down your words in your vocabulary book make sure you spell them correctly as they will serve as the basis for further work with the words.

Systematic word lists

Your word lists should not only contain the English words and their German translation, but most importantly, contexts in which the words are used, e.g. sentence examples and individual tips for learning. Therefore divide your lists into 4 columns as follows:

1st column	2nd column	3rd column	4th column
The new word or expression	The corresponding German word or expression	Example sentence **Tip!** Leave a gap where the new word should be. When revising your words you can fill in the gap.	Useful tips for learning, e.g. – collocations – synonyms/ antonyms – false friends – word pictures – …

Here is an example of how you can organise the word list of the lexical field "**Multi-cultural Britain**":

English	German	Example sentences	Useful tips
Commonwealth citizen	Bürger des Commonwealth		
to hold a British passport	einen britischen Pass besitzen		

English	German	Example sentences	Useful tips
to apply for … to refuse sb British citizenship	die britische Staatsbürgerschaft beantragen verweigern	Every year thousands of people officially ~ British citizenship.	application refusal ↔ to grant
immigration illegal immigration	Einwanderung illegale Einwanderung		immigrant to immigrate into
an influx/a wave/ a flow of immigrants	ein Einwanderungsstrom	GB has always experienced an enormous ~ of immigrants.	
to encourage immigration	Einwanderung unterstützen		= to promote immigration ↔ to discourage
to accept/to welcome immigrants	Einwanderer zulassen/ willkommen heißen		
asylum seeker to apply for asylum to grant asylum	Asylant um Asyl bitten Asyl gewähren		
refugee	Flüchtling	~ fleeing from the war poured into GB	an economic/political/ war/environmental refugee
to limit/to curb the number of immigrants	die Anzahl der Einwanderer begrenzen	As GB is not able to cope with the thousands of immigrants anymore the government is thinking about ~.	
to pass stricter laws	strengere Gesetze erlassen		= to tighten laws = to bring in/to impose restrictions ↔ to lift restrictions
to refuse entry	die Einwanderung ablehnen		
to deport immigrants deportation	Einwanderer abschieben Abschiebung		to return immigrants
to repatriate	in die Heimat zurückführen	Last year many illegal immigrants were forcibly ~.	to face forced repatriation

English	German	Example sentences	Useful tips
in search of/for … better opportunities in employment better education a higher standard of living more social security	auf der Suche nach … besseren Einstellungs-bedingungen besseren Bildungs-chancen einem höheren Lebensstandard größerer sozialer Absicherung		to search for sb/sth
persecution to persecute	Verfolgung verfolgen	A lot of immigrants are ~ for their religious beliefs.	to escape political or religious persecution
to assimilate into British society	sich in die britische Gesellschaft integrieren	Some immigrants, part-icularly the younger ge-nerations successfully ~.	= to integrate into
to provide cheap labour	billige Arbeitskräfte stellen		
to settle in urban areas	sich in städtischen Gebieten niederlassen		settlement
different ethnic minority groups	verschiedene ethnische Minderheiten	Today, GB is a country in which ~ live side by side.	
ethnic diversity	ethnische Vielfalt		
the transition to a multicultural society	der Übergang in eine multikulturelle Gesell-schaft	With many different groups living in GB, the country is experiencing ~.	
racial discrimination	Rassendiskriminierung	Not being accepted by everyone immigrants still have to face ~ today.	to suffer from discrimi-nation in e.g. education
to be discriminated against	diskriminiert werden	Young immigrants often feel discriminated against at school.	
racial prejudice	Vorurteil gegen andere Rassen		to be prejudiced against sb/sth
(racial) harassment	Schikane	A lot of immigrants have already been victims of ~.	to be harassed by sb
(racial) tension	Spannung		
racist	Rassist		

English	German	Example sentences	Useful tips
racial clash	rassistischer Zusammenstoß		
(race) riot	Aufruhr/Ausschreitungen/Krawall	Regularly ~ break out in areas where a lot of immigrants live.	
to experience disadvantages	Nachteile erfahren		to experience social and educational disadvantages
to be disillusioned with	desillusioniert sein		
to have problems of adaptation	Anpassungsprobleme haben		to adapt to sth/to adjust to sth
high unemployment rate	hohe Arbeitslosenquote	The ~ is very ~ among young immigrants.	to be unemployed/to be jobless
badly-paid jobs	schlecht bezahlte Arbeit		≠ well-paid jobs
poor housing	schlechte Wohnbedingungen		= bad housing conditions

Visualizing techniques

Apart from writing your words down in word lists you can organise them with the help of different visualizing techniques.

a) The association network

An association network represents all the words that come to your mind in connection with a keyword. This keyword is placed in the centre and all the other words are more or less systematically grouped around it.

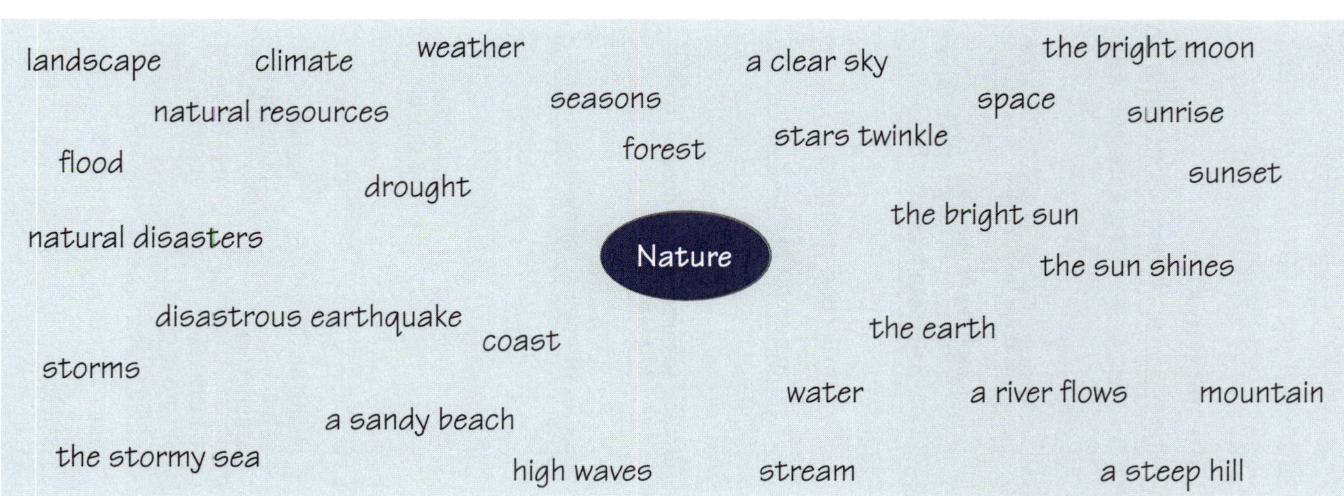

b) The mind map

A mind map represents words that are linked to a keyword. The keyword is placed at the centre and all the other words are arranged around it.

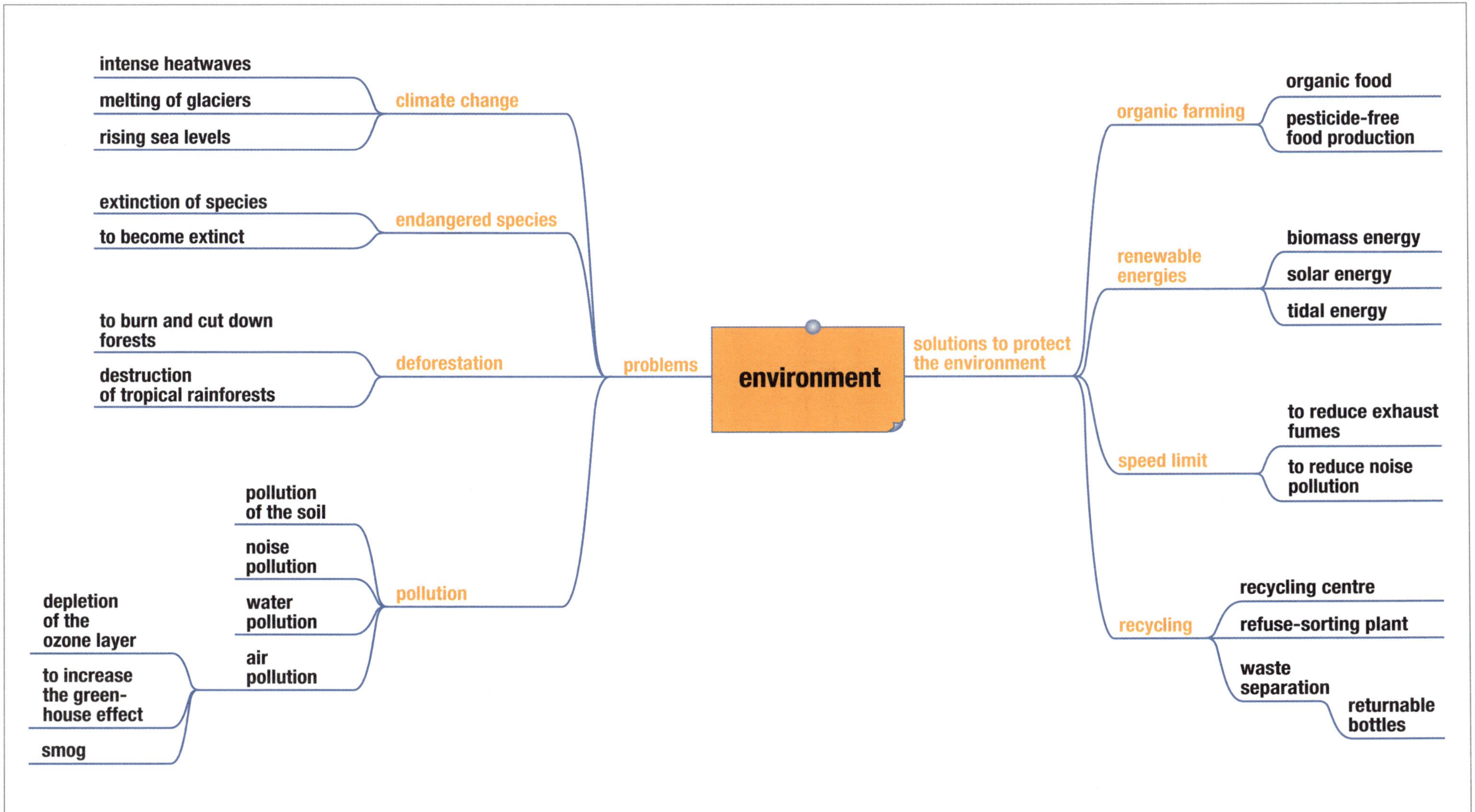

c) The flow chart

A flow chart is a schematic representation of a process, showing what comes first, second, third, etc. and last. The following flow chart includes vocabulary from the lexical field "global warming".

Causes

the burning of fossil fuels (oil, coal, natural gas)
to increase emissions of greenhouse gases
to deforest
deforestation
intensive farming
the use of fertilizers
to release greenhouse gases

↓

Effects

changes in global temperature
changes in weather patterns
heavy storms
extreme rainfall
intense heatwaves
severe drought
increase of desert land
forest fires
flash floods
rise of sea levels
mudslides
fast retreat of glaciers
contaminated water
spread of diseases
extinction of species
to be threatened with extinction
to be extinct
endangered species

↓

Solutions

the use of renewable energies: hydro power, wind power, solar power, biomass energy
nuclear energy
nuclear power station
carbon sequestration (= storage of carbon underground)
cap and trade (= trading of carbon emissions)
to reduce the burning of forests and fields
to recycle waste

d) The grid

A grid is a pattern of regular horizontal and vertical lines forming squares. The following grid includes words and expressions from the lexical field of "energy".

<table>
<tr><th colspan="6">Energy</th></tr>
<tr><td colspan="5">renewable energies</td><td>conventional energy</td></tr>
<tr><td>hydro energy</td><td>wind energy</td><td>solar energy</td><td>biomass energy</td><td>geothermal energy</td><td>nuclear energy</td></tr>
<tr><td>water</td><td>wind</td><td>sun</td><td>biological material, e. g. plant and animal material</td><td>the heat of the earth</td><td>Uranium
nuclear fission
nuclear chain reaction</td></tr>
<tr><td>hydro-electric power plant/ station
to build a dam
wave power plant/station
wave farm
tidal power plant/station
to build a tidal barrage
off shore turbine</td><td>wind farm
wind generators
wind turbine</td><td>solar thermal power plant/ station
solar cells
photovoltaic cell
solar panel</td><td></td><td>geothermal power plant/ station</td><td>nuclear power plant/station</td></tr>
<tr><td colspan="6">to generate energy
to supply energy</td></tr>
</table>

e) Other

Apart from the visual techniques represented above, your "visualizations" can take any form. You can organise them in form of a clock, a ladder, a time line, a word fork, etc.

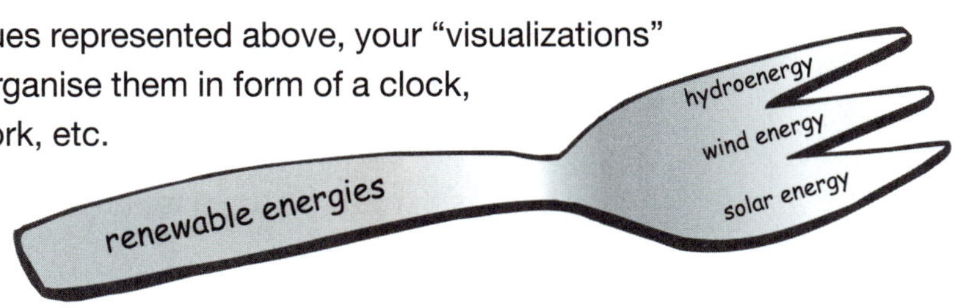

Tip! When resorting to visual techniques use colours, images, symbols, etc. to illustrate your visualizations.

How to work with your vocabulary book

- Only learn **a set of 7 +/– 2 words at a time**.
- When going through the words **for the first time have a look at the 3rd column with the example sentences first.** If you have left a gap, try to fill the gap with the appropriate word.
  Do you know how to spell it? → Write it down.
  Do you know how to pronounce it? → Say it aloud.
- **Check if you know the German equivalent.**
- Mark the words you do not know with a pencil.
- Have **a break**. Do something else. But do not watch TV or play on the computer!
- When revising the words **a second time start off with the German word in the 2nd column.**
  Do you remember the English word, its spelling, its pronunciation?
  Do you remember the example sentence?
  Do you remember any of the learning tips you have written down?
- Particularly check the words you did not know. Erase the markings if you remember them this time.
- **Revise the words regularly each time starting off with a different column.** The sequence of learning and review should become more spread out timewise (→ pp. 60 – 62).

Why you should keep a vocabulary book

It is true that keeping a vocabulary book requires a lot of self-discipline. But it is worthwhile for the following reasons:

- You can store a large number of words in one book.
- You can add new words or new word fields at any time.
- You can organise your words according to individually chosen principles.
- You can choose between different ways of writing down and illustrating your words.
- You can note down as much additional information as you need in order to learn your words.
- You actively work with the new words by organising them and writing them down.

NOW OVER TO YOU

- Here is a list of English words which have to do with "the media". Organise them in a systematic word list. Add more words and expressions connected to the topic.

communication	to publish	tabloid
phonecard	to surf the Internet	subscription fee
to send a letter	soap opera	entertaining
to communicate	sensational	documentary
parcel	a local call	to report on
a long-distance call	influence on	to design a website
to broadcast	picture	censorship
urgent	controversial	news magazine
radio	caption	mobile phone
feature	engaged	to censor sth
news	viewer	sources of information
to tune	headline	current affairs
postcard	commercial	data processing
fax machine	letter	to transmit
TV	photo	press
listener	quality newspaper	to subscribe to
editorial	to influence	to receive a letter
to become addicted to	to advertise	newspaper
readership	to inform about	popular newspaper
weather forecast	data protection	publication
advertisement	mass media	

(2) Word cards

Using word cards is another rewarding way of recording new words.

How to prepare word cards

- According to the number of words you want to learn prepare a set of small cards which are easy to carry (as a rule 20–50 cards).
- Write down on one side of the cards the words you want to learn. Check your spelling. Make sure you write legibly.
  Sometimes it is helpful to note down more information about the word, e.g. common collocations, synonyms and antonyms, example sentences, etc.
- On the other side of the cards write down the German translation.
  Instead of the German translation you can e.g. write down sentences with a gap, questions or else you can draw a picture. In fact, you can put down any key which helps you to recall the English word.
- In any case, keep the cards as simple as possible!

verschmutzen	to pollute
	to contaminate
	The air is increasingly polluted by exhaust fumes.

How to work with your word cards

- When going through the set of words you want to learn for the first time **look at each English word and try to remember its German meaning**.
- Then go through the word cards again and **check if you can recall the English word by having a look at the German translation or the sentence contexts, the questions, the pictures,** etc.
  Check the spelling and the pronunciation.
- Repeat this process.
- **Keep reshuffling the card pack** to avoid a serial effect, i.e. that one word triggers the recall of the next word.
- **Put difficult words near the beginning or the end** as words at the beginning and at the end of a set are remembered more easily.
- Having revised the set of words a couple of times, **take out the words you know**.
- **Add new items** you want to learn.
- And remember to space out your revision sessions (➔ pp. 60 – 62).

The vocabulary box

In order to revise your words more systematically with the help of word cards you can use a **vocabulary box**.

- Build a vocabulary box with 5–7 sections.
- The 1st section of the vocabulary box contains all the word cards with the new words.
- Revise your words as explained above. Put the words you know into the 2nd section. The words you cannot recall stay in the 1st section.
- After some time revise your words again, those in the 1st as well as in the 2nd section of your vocabulary box. Place the words you know from the 1st section into the 2nd section. Like before, the words you do not know remain in the 1st section. Place the words you know from the 2nd section into the 3rd section. The words you do not know go back into the 1st section. Continue this process with the remaining sections. As soon as the words can be placed into the last section remove them from the set of cards. You should actually be able to remember them without any problems.

– Increasingly space out your repetition sessions (➔ pp. 60–62).

For more word card activities see ➔ pp. 93–101.

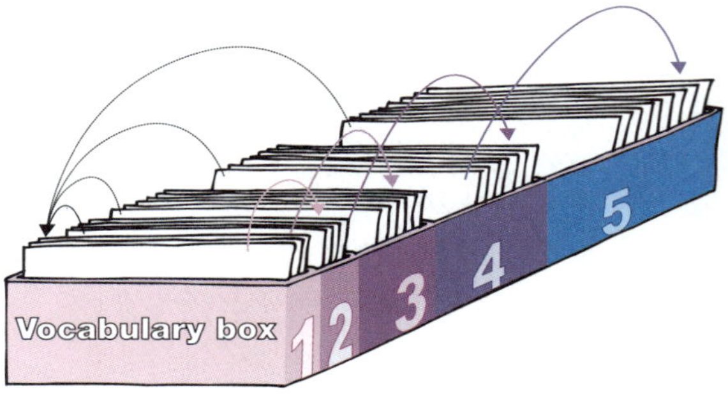

Why you should work with word cards

Working with word cards seems to be an efficient technique to learn words for the following reasons:

– Being able to take the word cards with you wherever you want means that you can revise your words at any time (e.g. when waiting for the bus).
– You can reorganise your words, i.e. sort out words you know, add new words and change the order of the words.
– You concentrate more on the words which are difficult for you to learn.
– Actually, seeing the number of words you have already learned working with word cards is a very motivating technique.
– There are a number of games you can play with your word cards.
– All in all, it is a very efficient technique in terms of feedback for the time you spent and the effort you made.

(3) Computer programmes for vocabulary

These days there are various computer programmes designed to promote vocabulary learning. Most of them put many of the principles of good vocabulary learning into practice. In fact, a lot of the programmes resemble a word box. The learner ideally supplies the words that go into the database. The way the computer programme then presents the words to the learner is similar to the way the words are presented when working with a word box (see above). In any case, the software keeps a record of the learner's progress and gives him/her the necessary feedback.

If you decide to work with a computer you should take into account the following aspects when choosing the appropriate software:

– Which words make up the database?
– Which aspects of the words are included in the learning and revision process?
– How are the words presented?
– What feedback is given and how are mistakes remedied?

REMEMBER

You can choose between various techniques to store words, the 3 main ones being
(1) the vocabulary book,
(2) word cards,
(3) computer programmes.
You can make use of all of them or you can choose only one depending on what you think is the most suitable technique for you.

How to expand your vocabulary

Learning a language first and foremost means learning new words. Therefore, you have to seek out as many opportunities as possible to encounter new words. You will learn actively some of the words you meet up with, others you will pick up incidentally.
Here are some possibilities where you might encounter new words:

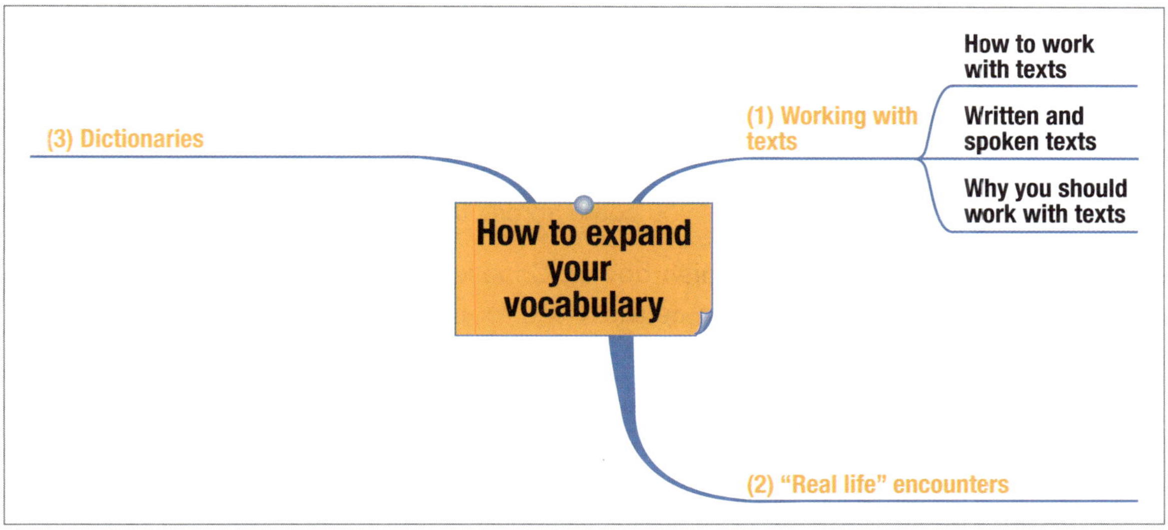

(1) Working with texts

How to work with texts

In order to enlarge your vocabulary, when working with a text you should proceed as follows:

– **Skim the text to get the gist of it.**
  What kind of text is it (e.g. a newspaper report, a literary text, a letter, an advertisement)?
  What is the text about?
  Who wrote it?
  Why did the author write it?
  What register is it written in (formal – neutral – informal)?

– **Highlight all the words and expressions you find useful.**
  Your choice will depend on what kinds of words and expressions you are looking for. You can e.g. look for words and expressions that all belong to the same lexical field or you can look for words and expressions belonging to the same word class.

– **If you are in doubt about the meaning of the chosen words consult a monolingual or a bilingual dictionary.**

– **Note down in your vocabulary book the words you personally find worth memorizing.**
  Remember to organise the words (➔ pp. 43 – 56).

– **Work with the words.** You will find a variety of tasks on ➔ pp. 93 – 101.

Written and spoken texts

You can either work with written or with spoken texts.

Written texts

- You can study **coursebook texts**. The coursebooks you use in class usually contain a variety of texts offering a great amount of carefully chosen words and expressions for you to learn.
- You can read **English newspapers and magazines**. When reading articles from a newspaper or magazine try to follow a particular news story over a certain period of time. In the course of time you will find that reading about the chosen topic and understanding it becomes easier as you come across the same words again and again.
- You can read **English books**. Choose books you like and read them extensively, i.e. not paying attention to details. Read for pleasure and not for information. It does not matter what they are about.
- If you find the original books too difficult to read, start off with so-called **Easy Readers**, i.e. books that have been simplified or that have explicitly been written to meet the needs of learners of English.
- You can browse the **Internet**. You will find a lot of interesting texts.

Spoken texts

- You can listen to **your teacher**. Generally, your teacher is a good source of spoken language. You can pick up a lot of so-called **classroom phrases** from him/her, e.g. *Open your books at page 38, please; Complete the network; Scan the text for …; What do you think about …?; I can see your point, but …; Could you explain that (again), please?; Have you finished yet? …*
  Furthermore, your teacher is also a source of useful forms of **interpersonal language**, e.g. *How are you feeling today?; What did you do yesterday?; Tell us about your weekend; I see; I understand; Oh really!; I can't believe it; Never mind; Don't worry; …*
- You can listen to the **English radio**.
- You can listen to **English songs**. Usually songs provide a rich source of new words and expressions. Have a look at the songs in their written form as well.
- You can listen to **English audio books**.
- You can watch **English TV programmes**. You can choose between a variety of programmes, e.g. the news, documentary reports, music videos, chat shows, comedy shows, soap operas, etc.
- You can watch **English movies** on DVD.
- You can listen to **English podcasts** on the Internet.
- You can go to **English theatre plays**, which are sometimes presented by international theatre groups.

Why you should work with texts

Any kind of text, whether written or spoken, is a very fruitful source of vocabulary input for the following reasons:

- In a (con)text words are **easier to understand**.
- In a (con)text words are **memorized more easily**.
- In a (con)text words are presented as **collocations** and with their **grammatical characteristics**.
- In a (con)text words can be found that belong to the **same lexical field**.

(2) "Real life" encounters

"Really" meeting people and communicating with them is one of the best ways of learning the English language.

- You can find yourself a **penfriend** or an **E-mate**.
- You can take part in **discussion groups** on the Internet.
- You can talk to **native speakers**. Look out for opportunities to talk to a native speaker in your hometown, e.g. in international community centres.
- You can **go abroad**, e.g. during your holidays or on an exchange.

Wherever or whenever communicating with other people either in written or in spoken form try to pick up as many words and expressions as you can. It is always helpful to carry on you a small **notebook** in which you can jot down the words and expressions which you think are important. You can later copy them into your vocabulary book and organise them (➔ pp. 43 – 56).

(3) Dictionaries

In general, dictionaries are an indispensable source of words. Find more information about how to work with a dictionary on ➔ pp. 83 – 92.

REMEMBER

In order to improve your knowledge of the English language you need to enlarge your vocabulary continuously. Here are some ideas as to what you can do to encounter new words:

(1) Work with written or with spoken texts of any kind.
(2) Seek out opportunities to meet people and communicate with them.
(3) Consult dictionaries when necessary.

NOW OVER TO YOU

■ Read the following text about organic food. Highlight all the words and expressions that belong to the lexical field "Organic food". Organise them in a systematic way or with the help of a visualizing technique (➔ pp. 69 – 72). Add more words and expressions connected to the topic. If you want you can use a dictionary.

Organic food helps revive fortunes of Europe's farmers

The organic revolution is sweeping across Europe, with the area of land dedicated to environmentally-friendly, pesticide-free food production more than doubling in the last decade.
Organic farming now accounts for more than 4 per cent of agricultural land in the EU, more than double its 1998 share, according to a new report from its official statistics agency, Eurostat.
And organic land is likely to make greater inroads, as the consumer appetite shows no sign of slowing. "Organic almost certainly will continue to grow and we think it's a good thing," Michael Mann, an EU agriculture spokesman said.
The growth is partly being driven by Europe's farmers, who are being undercut by produce imported from countries such as Brazil. For many farmers, organic foods are becoming a key way to reinvent their failing farms. [...]
Conscious of this ballooning market, agriculture ministers from the 27 member states agreed this week on a compulsory logo, to be introduced from 2009, designed to reassure consumers that they are getting the genuine article.
The logo guarantees that at least 95 per cent of ingredients are completely free of chemicals – and imports will be subject to the same rule. But it also permits up to 0.9 per cent from genetically-modified organisms, a level that has angered green campaigners.
"It is a total cop-out by the European Union – setting a level of 0.9 per cent could result in the creeping GM contamination of organic food," said Ben Ayliffe, of Greenpeace. "It should be 0.1 per cent."
"Go into any supermarket and they are bursting with organic food, while GM foods are conspicuous by their absence. That's because consumers don't want them!" he added.
In recent years, European consumers have shown themselves willing to pay more for organic produce, reflecting an aversion to chemicals and a growing preference for natural farming techniques over the high-intensity production that has been blamed for crises such as BSE and foot-and-mouth disease.
Recognising this fact, Brussels will now provide higher levels of subsidy for organic farming than that given to non organic fruit and vegetables.
The UK has been a leader in organic farming. In 2005, more than 600,000 hectares of the country's farmland were cultivated organically, putting it ahead of France, a country more than twice its size. Yet only 3.8 per cent of UK farmland was devoted to organic production, compared with 11 per cent in Austria. The Alpine nation has a reputation as a strong opponent of intensive and biotech farming, recently refusing to follow an EU ruling allowing a type of genetically-modified maize made by Monsato.
While the Eurostat report primarily compared the 15 nations that joined the EU before 2004, it also pointed out that some of the biggest organic farms now are to be found in newcomers Slovakia and Czech Republic.

Adam Mitchell and Rachel Shields, The Independent, 14.6.2007, p. 27

How to deal with mistakes

Just as important as it is to encounter new words it is also important to use the new words correctly. Of course, there is no learning of a language without making mistakes. But instead of regarding mistakes as a proof of your inability to use a language you should consider them as a chance to learn from them.
In order to learn from your mistakes systematically you should keep records of the mistakes you have made in tests, class tests or in any other kind of texts in a "mistake book" or "mistake file". When noting them down you should sort your mistakes according to the following 3 categories:
- **Spelling**
- **Grammar**
- **General usage**

The first category "**Spelling**" simply contains all spelling mistakes.

In the second category "**Grammar**" you list grammar mistakes, e. g.
- syntax,
- word order,
- questions,
- reported speech,
- article,
- tenses,
- negation,
- comparison,
- ing-forms,
- infinitives.

The third category "**General usage**" comprises all sorts of mistakes, e. g.
- words you used wrongly (e. g. similar words, false friends),
- prepositions,
- conjunctions,
- discourse phrases,
- phrasal verbs,
- collocations,
- idioms,
- register.

Divide your mistake lists up into 3 columns: spelling, grammar and general usage. Note down the corrected word or expression and its context in the appropriate column, clearly marking what has been corrected. Here is an example of how you can organise a mistake list:

At the moment the U.S. is experiancing a fundamental change in its demographic structure.
Coloured people are still discriminated today.
Being attracted by the land of unlimited opportunities Mi Len came in 1973 to America.
The Asians today are the most sucessfull immigrant group.
The newcomers were given a lot of informations.

Spelling	Grammar	General usage
… the U.S. is experiencing a fundamental change … Asians are the most successful immigrant group.	Mi Len came to America in 1973. → **Place before time!**	Coloured people are still discriminated against today. The newcomers were given a lot of information.

REMEMBER

By keeping records of your mistakes in a special "**mistake book**" or "**mistake file**" you make sure that you use your words correctly.

How to work with a dictionary

Dictionaries are an essential study aid when learning a language. When working with the dictionary you should know about the following aspects:

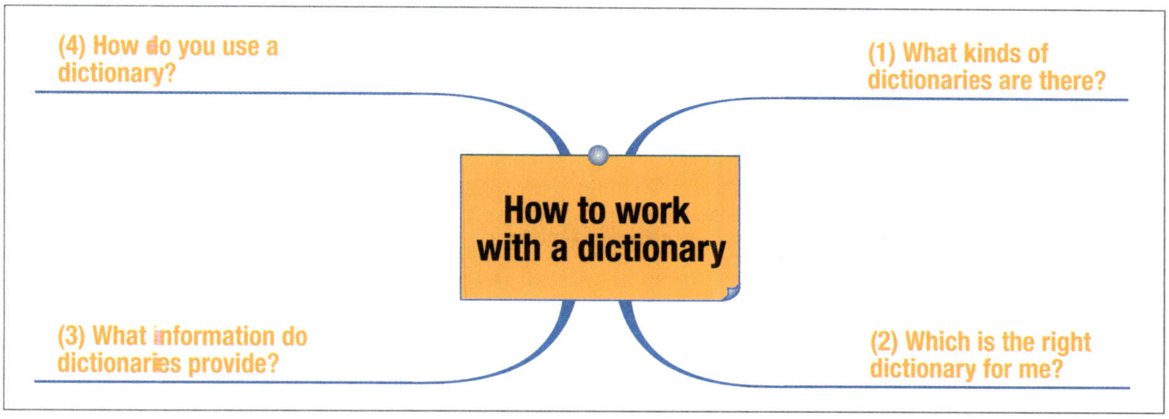

(1) What kinds of dictionaries are there?

There are many different kinds of dictionaries, the most important being monolingual and bilingual ones.

Monolingual dictionaries are written in one language, i. e. the headword and the information about the word is exclusively given in English. Monolingual dictionaries usually contain a whole range of information about a word (see below).

im·mi·gra·tion /ˌɪmɪˈɡreɪʃn/ *noun* [U] **1** the process of coming to live permanently in a country that is not your own; the number of people who do this: *laws restricting immigration into the US* ◇ *a rise/fall in immigration* ◇ *immigration officers*—compare EMIGRATION **2** (also **imˈmigration control**) the place at a port, an airport, etc. where the passports and other documents of people coming into a country are checked: *to go through immigration*

A. S. Hornby: Oxford Advanced Learner's Dictionary of Current English. Oxford, Oxford University Press, 2005

Bilingual dictionaries use two languages. Whereas the headword and possible examples are given either in German or in English, the meaning is given in the other language. Apart from giving the corresponding word in the other language, bilingual dictionaries generally contain additional information about the word itself.

German – English

Einwanderung <-, -en> *f* ■ **jds ~ nach/in etw** *akk* sb's immigration to/into sth

Pons Großwörterbuch für Experten und Universität. Stuttgart, Klett, 2001

English – German

immigration [ˌɪmɪˈɡreɪʃᵊn] *n no pl* ❶ (*action*) Einwanderung *f*, Immigration *f* ❷ (*immigration control*) Grenzkontrolle *f* ❸ AM (*immigration control*) ■ **~s** *pl* ≈ Grenzschutz *m* (*an Flughäfen*); **~s and customs** Bereich *m* der Personen- und Zollkontrolle (*auf Flughäfen*)

Pons Großwörterbuch für Experten und Universität. Stuttgart, Klett, 2001

Both, monolingual as well as bilingual dictionaries are indispensable aids when learning English.

Other dictionaries, which can be very helpful when learning a language, are e.g. **dictionaries of collocations, dictionaries of idioms, dictionaries of phrasal verbs, picture dictionaries** and so-called **vocabulary books**, in which words are organised thematically.

Dictionary of collocations

immigration *noun*

1 coming to live in a country
- ADJ. **illegal | large-scale, mass**
- VERB + IMMIGRATION **control, restrict** *laws restricting immigration into the US*
- IMMIGRATION + NOUN **control, law, policy, rules | authority, officer, official, service**
- PREP. **~from** *There was a sudden increase in immigration from Eastern Europe.*

2 (*also* **immigration control**) at a port/airport
- VERB + IMMIGRATION **go/pass through** *We landed at Heathrow and went through customs and immigration.*
- IMMIGRATION + NOUN **checks, formalities, procedures** *calls for tighter immigration procedures*

Oxford Collocations Dictionary for Students of English. Oxford, Oxford University Press, 2002

Picture dictionary

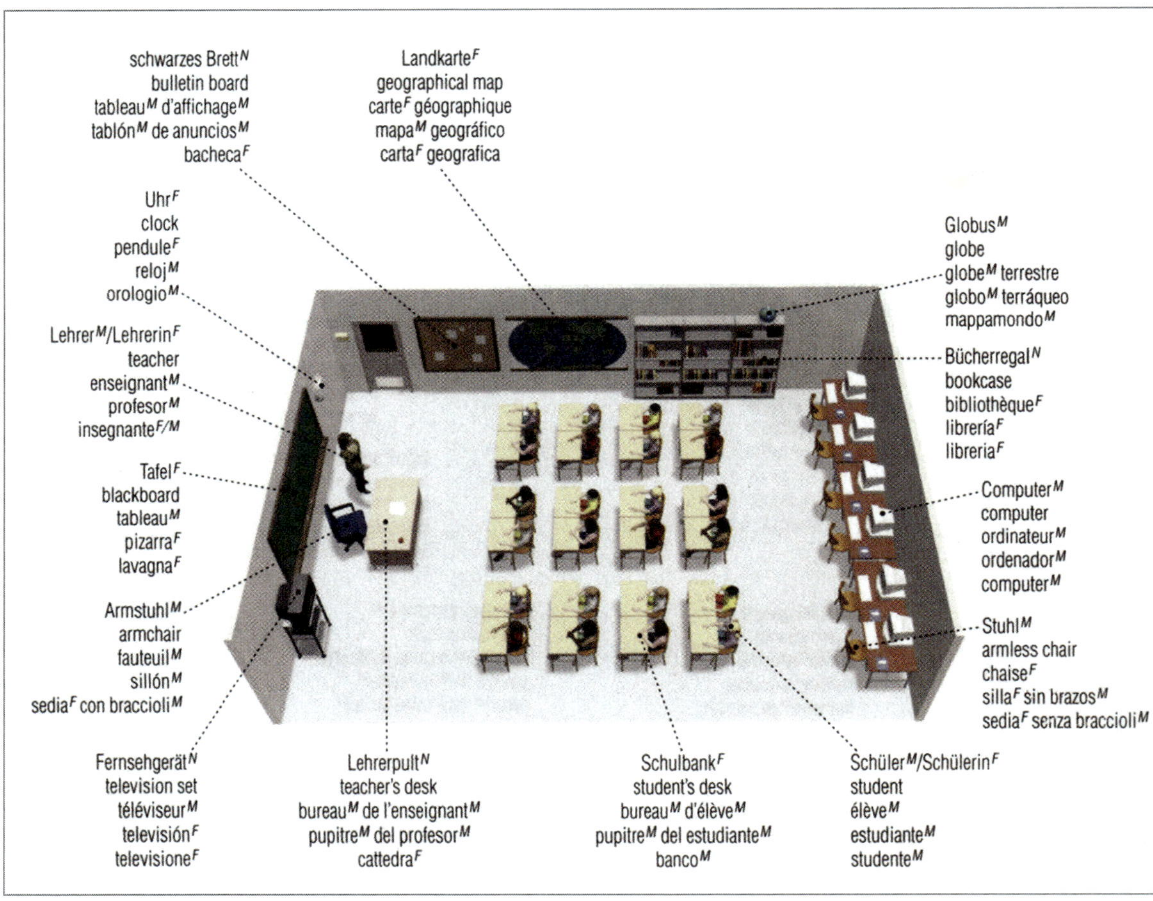

Pons Bilderwörterbuch, Stuttgart, Klett, 2003

Vocabulary book

8.2 Schule, Unterricht

school *n* [sku:l]	Schule
Do the Dawsons' children still **go to school?**	Gehen die Kinder der Dawsons noch zur Schule?
Pat **left school** when she was 16.	Pat verließ mit 16 die Schule.
at school	in der Schule
school exchange	Schüleraustausch

British schools

Age	School system	Exams
18		*A levels, AS levels, GNVQs*
17		
16	*4th assessment test*	*GCSEs*
15		
14	*3rd assessment test*	
13		
12	Secondary School	
11	*2nd assessment test*	
10		
9		
8		
7	*1st assessment test*	
6		
5	Primary School	

In Britain all children must attend school from the age of five to sixteen. 93% of all students in Britain go to a school in the **state school system**. 7% go to a school in the **independent school system (private school / public school)**.
All **state schools** and most **private/public schools** use the **National Curriculum**. Pupils are taught in English, mathematics, science, design and technology, information technology, history, geography, music, art, physical education and religious education.
At the ages of 7, 11, 14 and 16, pupils take national assessment tests in English, mathematics and science so that their individual level can be compared to national standards.
Pupils in the state school system generally attend **comprehensive schools** until they are 16 or 18. About 6% go to **grammar schools** which are **state schools** which only accept pupils who, at the age of 11, pass a special examination.
A **preparatory school** or **prep school** is a **private school / public school** that pupils start at the age of seven and then attend until they are 16 or 18.

private school *n* ['praɪvɪtˌsku:l]	Privatschule *(mit Schulgebühren)*
public school *n* ['pʌblɪkˌsku:l]	traditionsreiche Privatschule *(wie Eton und Harrow,* BE); öffentliche Schule (AE)
The independent school system in Great Britain consists of all private schools.	Das nichtöffentliche Schulwesen in Großbritannien besteht aus sämtlichen Privatschulen.
state school BE *n* ['steɪtˌsku:l]	staatliche/öffentliche Schule
state school system	öffentliches Schulwesen
pupil *n* ['pju:pl]	Schüler(in) (BE); Grundschüler(in) (AE)
schoolboy/schoolgirl BE *n* ['sku:lbɔɪ/'sku:lgɜ:l]	Schuljunge, Schüler / Schulmädchen, Schülerin
student *n* ['stju:dnt]	Student(in) (BE); Schüler(in), Student(in) (AE)
schoolchildren *n pl* ['sku:ltʃɪldrən]	Schulkinder, Schüler(innen)
teacher *n* ['ti:tʃə]	Lehrer(in)
course *n* [kɔ:s]	Kurs, Lehrgang
form BE; **grade** AE *n* [fɔ:m; greɪd]	Schulklasse
What form/grade are you in?	In welcher Klasse bist du?
class *n* [klɑ:s]	Unterricht(sstunde)
We've got an English class at 10 o'clock tomorrow.	Wir haben morgen um 10 Uhr Englisch.
beginners' class	Anfängergruppe, -kurs
evening class	Abendkurs
classmate *n* ['klɑ:smeɪt]	Klassenkamerad(in)
lesson *n* ['lesn]	Unterrichtsstunde
Tim **gives private lessons in** maths.	Tim gibt Privatunterricht/ Nachhilfestunden in Mathe.

Gernot Häublein, Recs Jenkins: Thematischer Grund- und Aufbauwortschatz Englisch. Stuttgart, Klett, 2000

(2) Which is the right dictionary for me?

When **choosing the appropriate dictionary** for your needs take into account the following aspects:

- Most importantly, it should **meet your individual needs.** Therefore, ask yourself what exactly you need the dictionary for, e. g. for listening, reading, speaking, writing, translating.
- It should **suit your level of English** as far as the **number of words** is concerned.
- The **individual word entries** should be **easy to find**.
- The **explanations** should **not be too complicated to find**.
- **Additional information**, e. g. examples, collocations, antonyms, synonyms should be given.
- The **information** given about each word should be **easy to understand** and **clearly structured**.
- If possible, there should be **pictures** to illustrate the words.
- As far as the size is concerned, the dictionary should be **easy to handle**.
- The **price** should be adequate.

(3) What information do dictionaries provide?

In order to **get to know your monolingual or bilingual dictionary** take a look at the first and the last pages. Apart from the individual word entries and their explanations dictionaries usually provide much more information.

NOW OVER TO YOU

■ What information is given? Tick the appropriate boxes.

	table of contents
	pronunciation table showing the different phonetic symbols
	guide to the entries giving a general description of how they are structured
	abbreviations used in the dictionary
	symbols used in the dictionary
	labels used in the dictionary (e.g. labels which describe the region or country (such as *BrE*, *AmE*, *AusE*), in which words are only or mainly used, or labels to describe words that are appropriate in a particular situation or show a particular attitude such as *literary, formal, informal, approving, disapproving* or labels to describe words from particular subject areas such as *business, law, medicine*)
	explanations of codes which describe the grammatical characteristics of an entry (e.g. [C] *countable*) or its verb patterns (e.g. [VN] *verb + noun phrase*)
	table of irregular verbs
	list of most frequently occurring words
	punctuation
	numbers
	rules of word formation
	a list of the most common prefixes and suffixes
	geographical maps
	geographical names
	common first names

■ Note down what other information is given in your dictionary:

____

____

____

____

____

Of course, the main part of a dictionary is made up of the individual word entries. They usually contain a **headword** and all the relevant **linguistic information** about this word. Depending on the word entry, information about the following aspects is given:

headword

How is the word **spelled** (including hyphenation)?

Sentence **examples** are given.

What **different meanings** does the word have?

What are the **grammatical characteristics** of the word?

How **frequently** is the word used? Does it belong to the high-frequency or low-frequency words?

Which **word class** does the word belong to?

How is the word **pronounced**?

What are **synonyms** of the word?

What **collocations** does the word have?

en·vir·on·ment 0‑‑ /ɪnˈvaɪrənmənt/ *noun* **1** [C,U] the conditions that affect the behaviour and development of sb/sth; the physical conditions that sb/sth exists in: *a pleasant* ***working/learning environment*** ◇ *An unhappy* ***home environment*** *can affect a child's behaviour.* ◇ *They have created an environment in which productivity should flourish.* ◇ *the political environment* ◇ *tests carried out in a controlled environment* **2 the environment** [sing.] the natural world in which people, animals and plants live: *the Department of the Environment* ◇ *measures to protect the environment* ◇ *pollution of the environment* ◇ *damage to the environment* **3** [C] (*computing*) the complete structure within which a user, computer or program operates: *a desktop development environment*

SYNONYMS

environment

setting • surroundings • background • backdrop • situation

These are all words for the type of place in which sb/sth exists or is situated.

environment the conditions in a place that affect the behaviour and development of sb/sth: *An unhappy* ***home environment*** can affect children's behaviour. ◇ *a pleasant* ***working environment***

setting a place or situation or a particular type, in which sth happens or exists: *The island provided an idyllic setting for the concert.*

surroundings everything that is around or near sb/sth: *The huts blend in perfectly with their surroundings.*

background the things or area that are/is behind or around the main objects or people that are in a place or picture: *The mountains in the background were capped with snow.*

backdrop (*formal*) the scenery surrounding an event; the things or area behind the main objects in a place: *The events took place against the dramatic backdrop of the Atlas mountains.*

situation (*rather formal*) the type of area or surroundings that a town or building has: *The town is in a beautiful situation in a wide green valley.*

PATTERNS AND COLLOCATIONS

- **in** (a/an) environment/setting/surroundings/situation
- **against** a/the background/backdrop (of sth)
- a (good, etc.) environment/setting/situation **for** sth
- (a/an) **new/unfamiliar** environment/setting/surroundings
- sb/sth's **immediate** environment/setting/surroundings
- (a) **dramatic** setting/surroundings/background/backdrop

A. S. Hornby: Oxford Advanced Learner's Dictionary of Current English. Oxford, Oxford University Press, 2005

Sometimes information is also given about the following aspects:
- What **connotations** does the word have?
- What are **antonyms** of the word?
- Is the word used in any **idioms**?
- What is the **register** of the word?
- Is it **British**, **American** or **Australian English**?
- What are **typical sources of mistakes**?
- …

NOW OVER TO YOU

■ Study the following word entry. What information is provided?

pol·lu·tion /pə'lu:ʃn/ *noun* [U]
1 the process of making air, water, soil, etc. dirty; the state of being dirty: ***air/water pollution*** ◇ *to reduce levels of environmental pollution* **2** substances that make air, water, soil, etc. dirty: *beaches covered with pollution* **3 noise/light ~** harmful or annoying levels of noise, or of artificial light at night

A. S. Hornby: Oxford Advanced Learner's Dictionary of Current English. Oxford, Oxford University Press, 2005

(4) How do you use a dictionary?

You normally use dictionaries for two purposes, either
– for **comprehension**, i. e. listening, reading and translating, or
– for **production**, i. e. speaking, writing and translating.

How to use dictionaries for comprehension
When listening or reading in English or translating English texts into German you may come across words you do not know.

– First of all, ask yourself if you can guess the meaning of the word (→ pp. 25 – 34).

– If not, decide whether the word is necessary to understand the context.

– If so, look up the word in either a monolingual or bilingual dictionary. Sometimes there is no separate entry for the word you are looking for. In this case, you can e. g. go through the sub-entries, look up words of the same word family or look out for differences in spelling.

– Read the explanation of the word and decide whether it fits into your context. Sometimes various explanations are provided. Read the different explanations and with the help of the additional information given in your dictionary, i. e. examples or grammar information, decide which explanation fits best into your context.

– When using a bilingual dictionary *cross-check* whether the explanation you have chosen is appropriate by looking it up in a German-English dictionary.

Example: When looking up the word "purpose" in the sentence *Our organization's purpose is to protect the environment*, the English-German dictionary provides a number of different explanations such as *Grund, Absicht, Ziel, Sinn, Zweck, Entschlossenheit, Erfolg,* etc. Choose the word you think fits best and look it up in the German-English dictionary to make sure you have chosen the right one.

How to use dictionaries for production
When speaking or writing in English or translating German texts into English you may need a dictionary for different reasons.
In case you do not know an English word proceed as follows:

– First of all, ask yourself if you can find another English word or expression to paraphrase the word you are looking for.

– If not, look up the word in a bilingual dictionary.

– If different explanations are given try to decide with the help of the additional information provided which one is most suitable for your purpose.

– Cross-check whether the explanation you have chosen is the best choice.

REMEMBER

Here are some aspects to consider when working with a dictionary:

(1) There are different kinds of dictionaries, the main ones being monolingual and bilingual.

(2) Choose the dictionary you want to work with carefully according to your needs.

(3) Different dictionaries provide different kinds of information.

(4) You can use dictionaries for comprehension purposes such as listening, reading and translation or for production purposes such as speaking, writing and translation.

NOW OVER TO YOU

Use your dictionary to answer the following questions.

■ Rank the following words in terms of frequency.

❶ sick – unwell – ill ______________________

❷ specific – peculiar – particular ______________________

■ Cross the odd one out as far as pronunciation is concerned.

❶ albeit – conceit – deceit ______________________

❷ soar – saw – sue ______________________

❸ daughter – laughter – slaughter ______________________

❹ swallow – blow – sow ______________________

■ Choose the correct pronunciation.

❶ [wuːnd] [waʊnd]
The watch has stopped though I **wound** it up half an hour ago.

❷ [baʊ] [bəʊ]
Robin Hood's men were armed with **bows** and arrows.

❸ [ˈmɪnɪt] [maɪˈnjuːt]
The engineer explained the machine in **minute** detail.

■ Which word classes do the following words belong to?

1. hollow ______________________
2. fine ______________________

■ Complete the table with the correct forms.

Verb	Noun	Adjective	Adverb
	protection		
		beautiful	
rely			
			carefully

■ Find out what the abbreviations stand for.

1. VIP ______________________
2. YMCA ______________________
3. BBC ______________________
4. MP ______________________

■ Decide which words fit best into the following sentences:

work – labour – toil – task – job – employment – duty

1. Your ______________ will include looking after the children.
2. The organisation is fighting against child ______________.
3. School leavers are finding it more and more difficult to find ______________.
4. This is a difficult ______________. I wonder if I can get it done today.
5. Every morning I go to ______________ at 8 o'clock.
6. She had a life full of hardship and ______________.
7. He lost his ______________ last month. Now he is unemployed.

■ Decide which word fits in which sentence.

1. **destiny – destination**

We arrived at our ______________ safe and sound.

It was his ______________ to die young.

2. **permit – permission**

You have to ask the teacher for ______________.

You're not allowed to park here without a special ______________.

❸ **self-conscious – self-confident**

She knows exactly what she wants. She is a ______________________________ woman.

He doesn't like speaking in front of many people. He is very _______________________.

❹ **convinced – convicted**

I'm ___________________________ he is not guilty.

He was ___________________________ of murder.

■ Find the opposites (antonyms) of the following words.

❶ important ____

❷ adequate ____

❸ legible ____

❹ smoker ____

■ Match the following words.

odds
give law
out sooner
back

and/or

later
order forth
ends about
take

■ Complete the following idiomatic expressions.

❶ Susan is head and ____________________ above the rest of the girls.

❷ She has got a ____________________ on her shoulder.

❸ She is a bit of an odd-___________.

❹ I was scared ____________________.

■ Find out which of the following verbs take the -ing-form and which take the to-infinitive.

❶ (to) consider ____

❷ (to) admit ____

❸ (to) promise ____

❹ (to) mind ____

■ Fill in the correct prepositions in the following sentences.

❶ She had difficulties ________ finding her way home.

❷ I'm tired ________ waiting any longer.

❸ I don't see any possibility ________ coming to the party tonight.

❹ This is a nice example ________ Greek history.

■ Match the following phrasal verbs with the appropriate meaning.

I must be **seeing** things.	not be deceived by
I must **see to** my homework.	accompany sb who is about to set off on a journey
They've gone to **see** Jane **off** at the station.	deal with
It's difficult to **see through** his behaviour.	have hallucinations

■ Find the plurals of the following nouns.

1. crisis ______
2. supply ______
3. information ______
4. phenomenon ______

■ Find the forms of the past tense and the past participle of the following verbs.

Infinitive	Past tense	Past participle
to light		
to hit		
to kneel		
to dig		

■ What are the British equivalents of the following American forms?

1. sidewalk ______
2. restroom ______
3. vacation ______
4. truck ______

■ With your friends play the following dictionary game:
From a monolingual dictionary choose a word you do not know, e.g. to lavish. While the one having chosen the word writes down the definition given in the dictionary all the others write down their own definition. Collect the definitions and read them out aloud. Which definition is closest to the correct one? Finally read out the correct definition. The player whose definition has come closest to the correct one will get a point.

How to use your words

Use them or lose them! – There is no doubt that learning and eventually memorizing new words implies using them, i. e. working with them. Different kinds of media such as books, computer programmes, board games, etc. offer a vast variety of vocabulary exercises, which have been designed to do just that.
The following choice of vocabulary games can only give you an idea of what you can do to work with a set of words you want to learn and memorize.
Some of the games you can play on your own. For others you will need a partner or a group of players.

Vocabulary games

Hangman

Number of players: 2 and more

Activity: One of you thinks of a word and draws – on a sheet of paper – as many dashes as the word contains. The other player tries to guess the word by suggesting letters. If he/she comes up with a letter that occurs in the word, the letter is written down in the space where it occurs. If the letter doesn't occur in the word an element of the "hangman's diagram" is drawn. If the other player guesses the word before the drawing is completed he/she wins. If the drawing is completed before he/she can guess the word he/she loses.

How many words are there in ...?

Number of players: 1 and more

Activity: Choose any word from your list and try to form as many words as possible with the letters from your chosen word. You can use the letters repeatedly, but only once in a word.
If you play the game with a partner compare the words you have found. The one who has found most of the words wins.

Example: IMMIGRATION
no – not – nor – on – am – tan – tin – tag – gram – grit – grin – groan – rat – ration – ration – rating – mat – grant – migrant – trim – trio – train – tram – torn, etc.

NOW OVER TO YOU

■ How many words are there in the word "Commonwealth"?

Write an acrostic

Number of players: 1 and more

Activity: Choose any word from your list and write an acrostic. Try to find words having to do with the topic. Make up a story with the words found.
If you play the game with a partner compare your stories and decide which one is best.

Example:

I	ndia
M	ulticultural
M	ix
I	llegal
G	overnment
R	acial
A	ssimilate
T	ension
I	ntegrate
O	pportunity
N	ationality

NOW OVER TO YOU

- Write an acrostic with the word DISCRIMINATION and write a short text which contains all the words you have found.

Memory

Number of players: 1 and more

Activity: In order to play *Memory* you need a set of 20–40 word cards with the words you want to learn and another set of cards on which you write down keys that will help you to learn the words of the first set. As keys you can use

- the German translation,
- the phonetic transcription,
- a synonym,
- an antonym,
- a hyponym,
- a meronym,
- a definition,
- a paraphrase,
- a phrase with a gap to be filled in,
- a picture.

Spread the cards on a table, face down, and try to find corresponding pairs of word cards by turning two cards at a time. Continue until you have found all corresponding words.
If you play the game with a partner count the number of pairs each of you has found. The one having found the greatest number of pairs is the winner.

Kim's game

Number of players: 1 and more

Activity: In order to play *Kim's game* you need a set of 20–40 word cards with the words you want to learn. Spread the cards on a table, study the words for about 1 minute, cover them up and try to remember as many words as possible.
If you are playing with a partner ask your partner to take away a certain number of word cards while you look away. Try to remember which cards are missing.

Guess my word

Number of players: 2 and more

Activity: In order to play *Guess my word* you need a set of word cards with the words you want to learn. From your stack of word cards take one card at a time and make your partner guess the word by explaining it to him/her in words, without using the word on the card, or else by drawing the word or miming it. As soon as your partner has guessed the word, pick up a new card. If he/she cannot guess the word, put the card aside and pick up a new one. Set a time limit of 1 minute. The player who has guessed most of the words within the given time limit wins.

The coffeepot game

Number of players: 2 and more

Activity: In order to play *The coffeepot game* you need a set of word cards with the words you want to learn. Pick up a word card. Your partner has to guess the word by asking yes/no questions about the word, the word *coffeepot* replacing the unknown word.

Examples: Do you *coffeepot* every day?
Do young people like *coffeepotting*?
Do you *coffeepot* at home?
Is a *coffeepot* an animal?

Set a time limit or limit the number of questions he/she is allowed to ask. Count the words he/she is able to find within the time limit. The player who has guessed the greatest number of words wins.

Who finds the word first?

Number of players: 3 and more

Activity: Spread word cards on a table. Choose a word and try to make the rest of the group guess the word you have chosen by explaining it, by drawing or by miming it. The player who has found the word card with the word you have chosen first can keep it. At the end of the game, the player who has collected most cards wins.

Categorize words

Number of players: 1 and more

Activity: Try to categorize the words of your word list according to given criteria.
If you are playing with a partner explain to him/her why you have categorized the words as you have. Here are some ideas as to which criteria you can categorize your words:

hot – cold	happy – sad	small – large
masculine – feminine	black – white	strong – weak
good – bad	square – round	clean – dirty
sweet – sour	slow – fast	night – day

Example:

sweet	sour
to hold a British passport to encourage immigration to welcome immigrants in search of better opportunities	illegal immigration a war refugee deportation to face social disadvantages

NOW OVER TO YOU

- Choose any of the above categories and group the words of the word list "Multicultural Britain" according to your chosen category.

What have they got in common?

Number of players: 1 and more

Activity: In order to play *What have they got in common?* you need a set of word cards with the words you want to learn. Take 3 words at random and try to find what they have got in common, e.g. they are all small, they are all white, they all contain the letter e, they all refer to an activity outside, they are all loved by children, they can all be eaten …

Associations

Number of players: 1 and more

Activity: In order to play *Associations* you need a set of word cards with the words you want to learn. Pick up – at random – a card from your pile of word cards and write down as many words you associate with the word as you can.
If you play with a partner you can compare the number of words the two of you have found within a given time limit. The player who has found the greatest number of words wins.

Create a sentence

Number of players: 1 and more

Activity: In order to play *Create a sentence* you need a set of word cards with the words you want to learn. Group your words into verbs and nouns. Take a word card from your stack of verbs and a word card from the stack of nouns. Create sentences by using the words you have picked up.

Create a story

Number of players: 1 and more

Activity: To play *Create a story* you need a set of word cards with the words you want to learn. Take a word card from your pile of cards and start creating a story by using the word you have picked up. Continue the story by picking up more word cards one at a time, using the words in your story.
If you play with a partner take it in turns to take a word card and to create a story.

Puzzles

Number of players: 1 and more

Activity: Create and do a puzzle with the words of your word list (→ examples on pp. 105 – 106).

NOW OVER TO YOU

- Cut out and mix the pieces of the puzzles "Multicultural Britain" on → pp. 105 – 106. Do the puzzles.

A word search puzzle

Number of players: 2 and more

Activity: Create a word search puzzle for your partner in which words from your word list are hidden. Then swap your word search puzzles with the ones of your partner and look out for the words he/she has hidden.

NOW OVER TO YOU

- Look out for 10 words in the following word search puzzle containing words on the topic "Multicultural Britain".

G	R	A	G	H	J	B	J	K	T	I	C	A	Q	R	H	G	J	K	G
P	A	I	M	M	I	G	R	A	T	I	O	N	H	J	K	T	K	Z	D
F	R	A	D	H	B	M	D	K	T	R	M	E	I	K	R	J	K	H	K
C	H	E	E	Y	H	V	R	F	H	V	M	S	Y	E	I	A	N	N	S
H	A	A	J	I	E	G	A	S	Z	O	O	Z	G	I	L	J	O	D	N
I	G	E	M	U	G	H	Q	E	R	T	N	S	A	F	O	I	I	C	F
L	V	G	E	W	D	G	J	K	B	N	W	C	R	I	T	S	T	A	E
N	M	B	E	E	D	I	F	G	H	Z	E	V	N	A	H	I	U	N	M
A	K	I	G	W	D	F	C	A	F	E	A	L	I	N	I	O	C	M	K
W	P	U	U	W	V	D	I	E	B	H	L	R	E	N	M	J	E	G	U
E	I	N	F	L	U	X	W	N	M	H	T	Z	I	O	K	P	S	M	L
F	S	A	E	W	R	G	U	I	O	A	H	A	H	S	N	H	R	T	H
JV	R	V	R	Y	V	F	W	B	P	E	C	H	J	F	R	S	E	E	O
H	A	N	S	W	D	E	G	E	G	J	I	T	E	V	J	N	P	Y	D
J	H	X	G	J	T	B	R	T	J	E	T	O	H	Z	T	D	E	G	J
K	V	M	E	E	K	Z	S	H	T	C	I	R	T	S	E	R	T	E	K
L	J	L	G	G	J	H	T	A	W	O	Z	A	G	Q	R	I	G	S	G
T	P	O	A	A	S	Y	L	U	M	S	E	E	K	E	R	G	P	A	R
I	M	D	J	N	I	L	G	U	K	S	N	B	H	E	G	J	Z	H	E
E	T	H	N	I	C	D	I	V	E	R	S	I	T	Y	M	M	O	J	W

Half a crossword

Number of players: 2 and more

Activity: Create *Half a crossword* including some of the words of your word list (see example below). Each of you has got an incomplete crossword. By asking for a word (*What's 5 down? What's 13 across?*) and by giving explanations try to fill in the missing words.

NOW OVER TO YOU

■ With your partner do the *Half a crossword* below.

Partner A

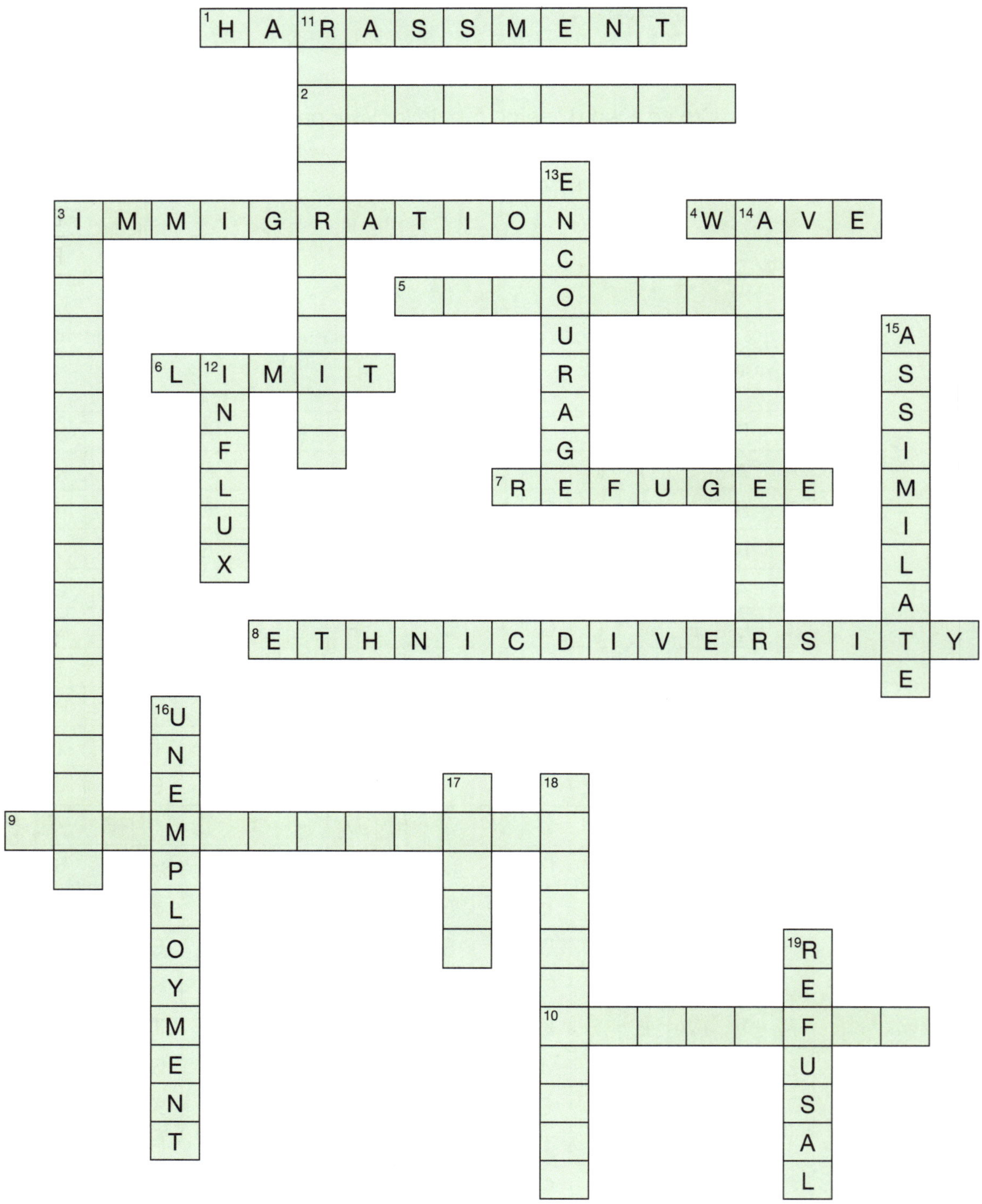

Partner B

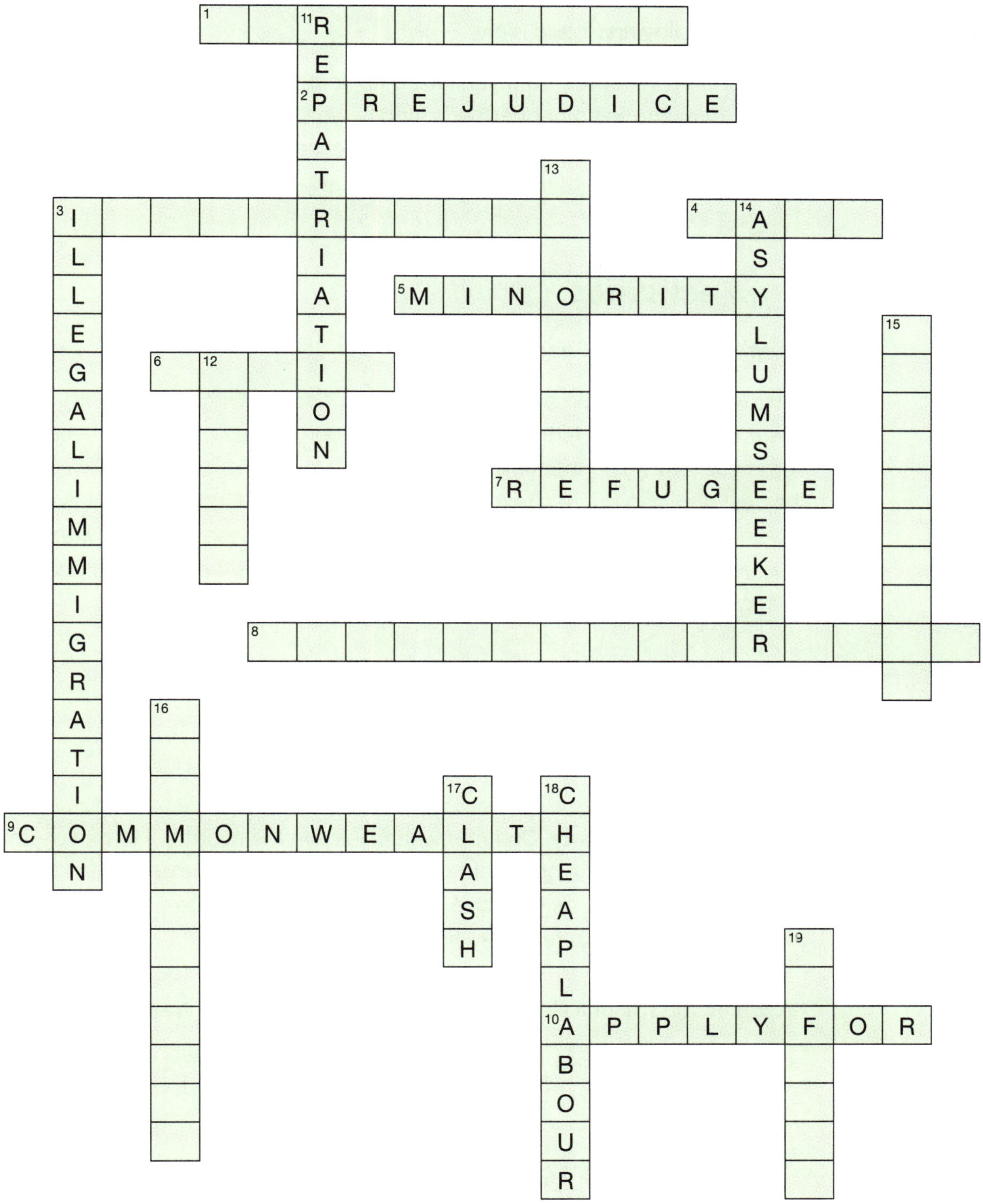
2 PREJUDICE
3 ILLEGAL IMMIGRATION
5 MINORITY
7 REFUGEE
9 COMMONWEALTH
10 APPLY FOR
11 REPATRIATION
14 ASYLUM SEEKER
17 CLASH
18 CHEAP LABOUR

Word battleships

Number of players: 2 and more

Activity: Hide 10 words from your word list in a 12 x 12 grid. Taking it in turns you and your partner try to find the other partner's hidden words by asking for the letter in a square (*What's the letter in B 8?*). As soon as one of you thinks he/she knows the hidden word, say it, indicating the exact position of the word. The one having first found all the words is the winner.

Cloze activities

Number of players: 1 and more

Activity: Choose a text on the topic you are dealing with. Delete parts of the text. You can delete e.g. individual letters (e.g. all vowels) or whole words (e.g. every 5th word or all the words you find worth memorizing).
The best way to prepare a text is to use the computer. Of course, you can use some whiteout to delete the words. Another method is to use confetti (easily made with your hole-puncher), which you can spread over your text, covering parts of the text at random.
Having prepared a text in this way try to fill in the gaps.

NOW OVER TO YOU

- Try to fill in the gaps in the following text on migration to and from Great Britain.
  Fill in the following words:

  to settle – to head for – Commonwealth – leave the country – to move – to increase – asylum seekers – nationals – to make the move – to experience – immigration – opportunities – figures – abroad – immigrant – to emigrate – incomers – influx – record – figures – nations – to return – living

A day in the life of a shifting population: the 2,500 migrants who come in and out

Up to 500 Britons a day are acting on their dreams of upping sticks and ______________ ___ to a new home. ______________ numbers ______________ from the UK last year, with Australia, Spain and France topping the list of preferred destinations.

The scale of the exodus emerged yesterday as government ______________ painted a dramatic picture of "departure lounge Britain". Some 1,500 ______________ arrived in the UK every day in 2005, with people from Poland leading the ______________, while 1,000 left the country.

Half of them were UK ______________, opting for a life ______________, mainly attracted by work ______________, a lower cost of ______________, and the prospect of retirement in warmer climates. One in five ______________ for Australia, where many Britons already have relatives, research by the Office for National Statistics showed. Large numbers also ____________________ to Spain, where a large expatriate retirement community lives, and France, which has surged in popularity with Britons over the past decade.

Thousands also chose the United States, which is recovering in popularity since the September 11 terrorist attacks, and New Zealand.

Of the other nationalities that left Britain last year, 56,000 were from the EU; 40,000 from "old ____________________" countries such as Australia, New Zealand and South Africa; 24,000 from "new Commonwealth" __________________ and 62,000 from other countries.

The UK, in common with much of the Western world, has ____________________ high levels both of _____________________________ and emigration for a decade. The numbers settling in this country for at least 12 months fell slightly last year to 565,000, with Poles representing the single largest group of _________________. Over the same period, 380,000 people ___________________________________, – half of them foreign nationals and half of them Britons emigration abroad. [...]

In 2005, 80,000 east Europeans settled in Britain, mainly from Poland. This was the first full year of the European Union membership of eight former Soviet-bloc countries. At the same time, 15,000 east Europeans __________________ home, suggesting that the numbers from those countries in Britain __________________, by 65,000 over the year.

The __________________ also confirm that the vast majority of east European workers who come to the UK [...] stay in the country for less than a year.

High numbers of immigrants came from south Asia last year, including India, Pakistan and

Bangladesh, as well as the "old Commonwealth" countries. And 15,000 Americans __________________ in Britain – mainly for work – while significant numbers of Spaniards and Germans also ________________________.

The net inflow of ______________________ fell to 11,000 from a record high of 81,000 five years earlier. It is the lowest figure for more than a decade.

Nigel Morris, The Independent, 3.11.2006, p. 5

How to cope with word gaps

It is only natural that as a learner of English you will regularly find yourself in situations where you cannot come up with the words you need to express what you want for different reasons. You have either learned the word, but in the meantime forgotten it again or you have actually not yet learned it.
Just as there are strategies to deal with unknown words when listening and reading in English (→ pp. 25 – 37), there are also strategies for you to make up for gaps in your vocabulary knowledge when speaking and writing in English.

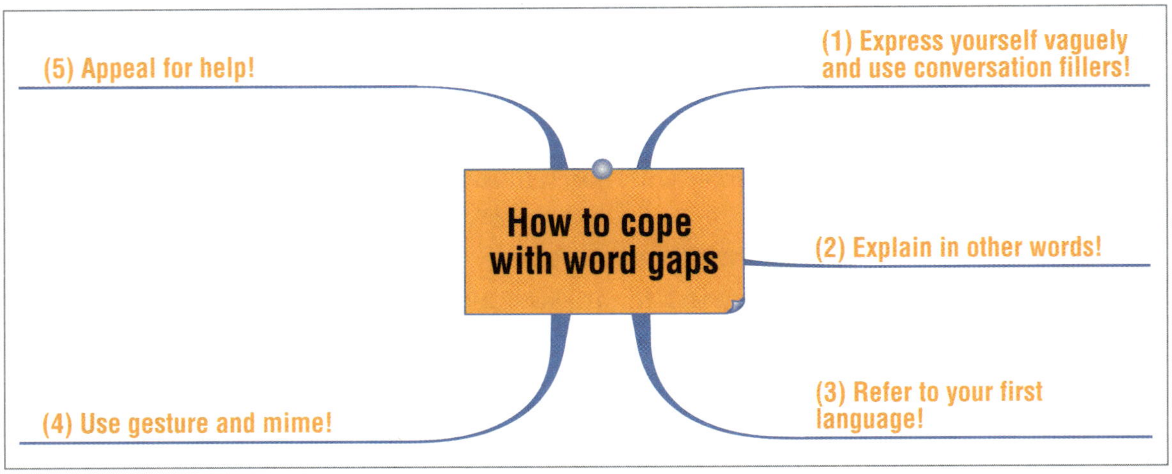

(1) Express yourself vaguely and use conversation fillers!

You can use vague words and expressions or conversation fillers in order to fill the gap.

Examples of vague words and expressions:

stuff/thing	whatever it is
a sort of/a kind of	thingummy
things like that	thingy
someone like that	whatisname

Examples of conversation fillers:

actually	in fact/as a matter of fact
you know/you see	I mean
er/um	how shall I put it
well	right

(2) Explain in other words!

You can explain the words you do not know in other words. There are different possibilities of doing this:

You can give a definition of the word.
Example: ***jemanden wütend machen*** – to make someone very angry (= to infuriate)
Dürre – a long period of time without rain (= drought)

You can paraphrase the word.
Example: ***Scheidung*** – when a man and a woman legally end their marriage (= divorce)
Fernglas – looking through it makes people and objects that are far away seem closer than they actually are (= binoculars)

You can give examples.
Example: ***Scham*** – you feel it when you have played a trick on your friend and you know it was a wrong and stupid thing to do (= shame)
Leiter, Wärter, Aufseher – people in charge of forests, youth hostels, churches, zoos, the traffic (= warden)

You can come up with synonyms or antonyms.
Example: ***heilloses Durcheinander*** – The presentation was a complete **shambles**.
= The presentation was a complete **mess**. (synonym)
≠ The presentation wasn't a **success**. (antonym)

You can provide hyponyms (= kind of) or meronyms (= part of).
Example: ***Werkzeug*** – a hammer, pliers, a screwdriver, a saw are … (= tools)
Fahrzeug – an engine, a steering wheel, tyres are parts of a … (= vehicle)

(3) Refer to your first language!

You can refer to your first language in different ways.

You can use the first language word, hoping that your partner will guess what you want to say.
Example: In how far are immigrants integrated into the British ***"Gesellschaft"***? (= society)
This chair looks really ***"gemütlich"***. (= comfortable/cosy)

You can "foreignise" a first language word, i. e. make it look and sound English.
Example: In the afternoon elderly ladies like to have a ***"coffee klatsch"***.
He loves sausages and ***"sourkraut"***.

You can give a literal translation of a first language word.
Example: ***Seefahrer*** – I would like to become a **"seadriver"** (= sailor).
Nachkommen – Having so many children she has a lot of people **"coming after her"** (= descendants).

(4) Use gesture and mime!

You can use gesture and mime to demonstrate what you want to express.

Example: ***etwas verabscheuen*** (= to detest something/someone)
riesig (= huge)

(5) Appeal for help!

You can ask your partner to help you find the word you are looking for.

Examples: Excuse me, I'm afraid my English is very poor. Is it correct to say …?
What do you say if you want to …?
What is it called in English?
What's the English word for …, please?
Do you understand what I want to say?
How do you spell this word?
How do you pronounce this word?

NOW OVER TO YOU

■ Find a way of explaining the following words.

1. *Bankfiliale* ______________________________
____
2. *Humbug* ______________________________
____
3. *Nikolaus* ______________________________
____
4. *Gelatine* ______________________________
____

REMEMBER

Here are the main strategies to help you cope with vocabulary gaps:

(1) You can express yourself vaguely or use conversation fillers.
(2) There are different ways of explaining the word if you do not know the English equivalent. You can e.g. come up with a definition, a paraphrase, examples, synonyms or antonyms, hyponyms or meronyms.
(3) You can refer to your first language by simply using the German word, by "foreignising" the German word or by literally translating the German word.
(4) You can use gesture and mime.
(5) You can appeal for help.

Multicultural Britain – A puzzle (1)

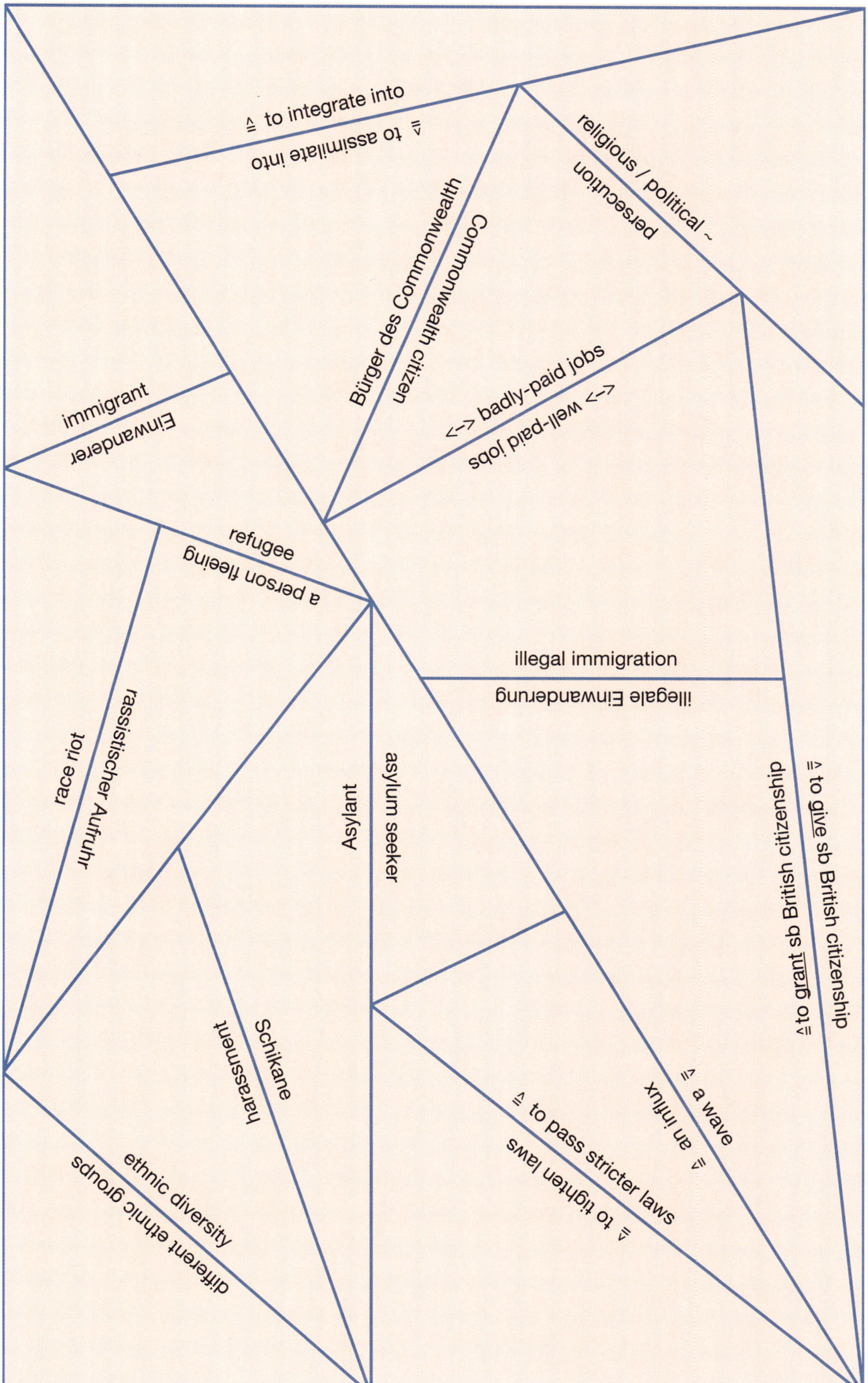

Multicultural Britain – A puzzle (2)

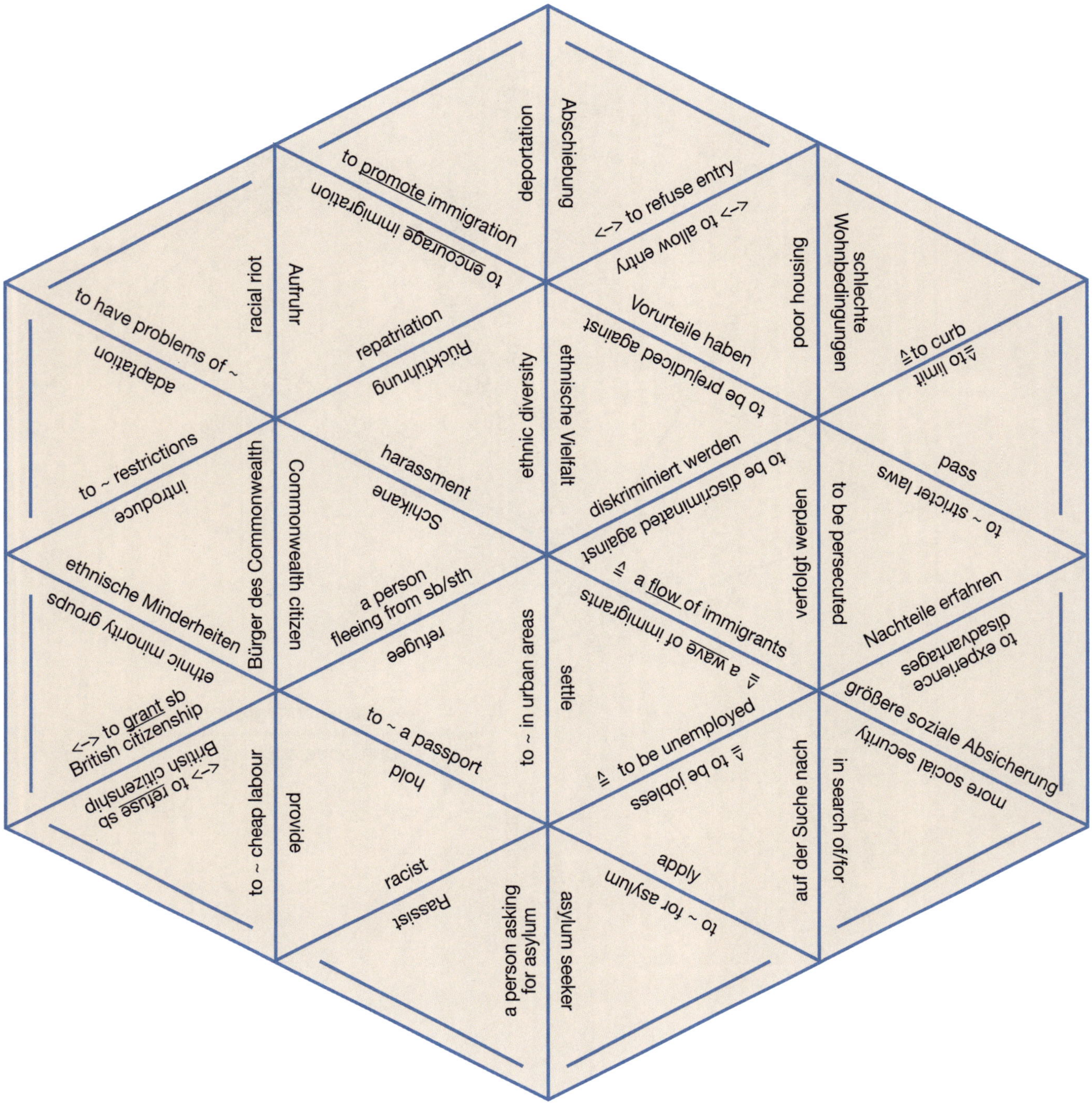

POWER PACK ENGLISH

Skills and strategies for advanced learners

Herausgegeben von Klaus Hinz
Erarbeitet von Klaus Hinz, Herbert Holtwisch und Karl Heinz Wagner

124 S., vierfarb., zahlr. Abb., kart., mit 23 S. Lösungen

Best.-Nr. **040 480 8**

Im modernen, selbstverantwortlichen Fremdsprachenunterricht ist die Beherrschung von *study skills* und *learning strategies* eine wichtige Voraussetzung für die Effizienz des Lernprozesses. Viele Lehrerinnen und Lehrer stellen jedoch gerade in diesem Bereich bei ihren Schülerinnen und Schülern in zunehmendem Maße Defizite fest.

Power Pack English führt nach neuesten lernpsychologischen Erkenntnissen prozessorientiert sowohl in den Umgang mit schriftlich vorliegenden und medial vermittelten Texten als auch in das Verfassen von Texten unterschiedlicher Art ein. Das jeweilige Verfahren wird an einem Beispiel detailliert exemplifiziert und kann in einer Anschlussaufgabe von den Schülerinnen und Schülern praxisnah angewandt werden. Mit dem beiliegenden Lösungsheft kann die richtige Lösung der Übung von den Schülern eigenständig kontrolliert werden.

POWER PACK ENGLISH

Project-oriented methods for advanced learners

Herausgegeben von Klaus Hinz
Erarbeitet von Klaus Hinz, Herbert Holtwisch, Elisabeth Mies, Gisa van Els und Karl Heinz Wagner

132 S., vierfarb., zahlr. Abb., kart.

Best.-Nr. **041 261 2**

Die Richtlinien aller Bundesländer betonen immer wieder die Eigenverantwortlichkeit der Schülerinnen und Schüler bei der Gestaltung ihrer Lernprozesse, weil auf dieser Grundlage eine motiviertere Einsatzbereitschaft als in einem lehrerzentrierten Unterricht beobachtet wird.

Das vorliegende Buch greift diese Forderung mit drei Unterrichtseinheiten auf, die nach neuartigen Prinzipien schüler- und produktorientiert aufbereitet sind und zur Projektarbeit hinführen.

Bildungshaus Schulbuchverlage
Westermann Schroedel
Diesterweg Schöningh Winklers GmbH
Postfach 2540 • 33098 Paderborn

Schöningh

Informationen zum Nulltarif
☏ 08 00 / 1 81 87 87
info@schoeningh-schulbuch.de
www.schoeningh-schulbuch.de

Solutions

How a word is made up

p. 8

■ Cross out some letters and find the hidden words. The words to be found have at least four letters. You don't have to change the order of the letters.

flower
love
comment
advertisement

■ Find the right order of the jumbled letters.

judgement
burglary

■ Fill in the missing letters.

sp**ee**ch
coll**ea**gue
simultan**eou**s
cons**cien**tious

p. 9

■ Find the corresponding British or American spellings.

British English	American English
colour	**color**
metre	meter
traveller	**traveler**
favourite	favorite
defence	defense
judgement	**judg(e)ment**

p. 11

■ Look at the following words. Decide where the main stress is.

/'honourable/ /ex'travagant/
/sur'prise/ /to con'sult/
/de'mocracy/ /'record/
/refu'gee/

p. 13

■ Match the sounds and the words.

embarrassed [ɪm'bærəst]
escape [ɪ'skeɪp]
separate ['seprət]
forward ['fɔːwəd]
kind [kaɪnd]
unavoidable [ˌʌnə'vɔɪdəbl]
package ['pækɪdʒ]
doctorate ['dɒktərət]
circumstance ['sɜːkəmstəns]

■ Find out with the help of a dictionary how the following words are pronounced.

February	[ˈfebruəri]
derogatory	[dɪˈrɒɡətri]
advertisement	[ədˈvɜːtɪsmənt]
yacht	[jɒt]
appreciate	[əˈpriːʃieɪt]
knee	[niː]
efficient	[ɪˈfɪʃnt]
delicious	[dɪˈlɪʃəs]

■ How are the following words pronounced? Match them with the corresponding phonetic symbol.

tough	[ʌ]
through	[uː]
rough	[ʌ]
dough	[əʊ]
borough	[oʊ]
cough	[ɒ]
nought	[ɔː]
plough	[aʊ]
enough	[ʌ]
ought	[ɔː]

p. 14 ■ Read out the following sentences. Mind the pronunciation of the words in bold letters.

❶ Since there is no time like the **present** [ˈpreznt], she thought it was time to **present** [prɪˈzent] the **present** [ˈpreznt].

❷ The bandage was **wound** [waʊnd] around the **wound** [wuːnd].

❸ We have to **wind** [waɪnd] up the kite string before the **wind** [wɪnd] gets too strong.

❹ The soldiers decided to **desert** [dɪˈzɜːt] their **dessert** [dɪˈzɜːt] in the **desert** [ˈdezət].

❺ There was a big **row** [raʊ] in the first **row** [roʊ] of the cinema.

❻ I won't shed a **tear** [tɪə(r)] if you **tear** [teə(r)] my old shirt into pieces.

■ Choose the right word to fill the gaps.

❶ Come **here** and sit down next to me.
Did you **hear** the latest news?

❷ A lot of animals hide during the day, but come out at **night**.
It was an honour to be one of King Arthur's **knights**.

❸ We are going to spend our holidays near the **sea**.
What can you **see** when looking through the hole?

❹ What is the **weather** like?
I am not sure **whether** I should ask him if he wants to go with me out tonight.

❺ I cannot see her anymore. She is out of **sight**.
Because of the building **site** there is a traffic jam on the M25.

❻ They are demonstrating for **peace**.
Would you like to have another **piece** of cake?

❼ Check the **brake** before you go on holiday.
I definitely need a **break** after this tiring working week.

❽ Stop **staring** at me. You are making me nervous.
Mind the **stair**.

p. 16 ■ Find out the meaning of the following words. What connotations do they carry? Try to find out if there are any intercultural differences.

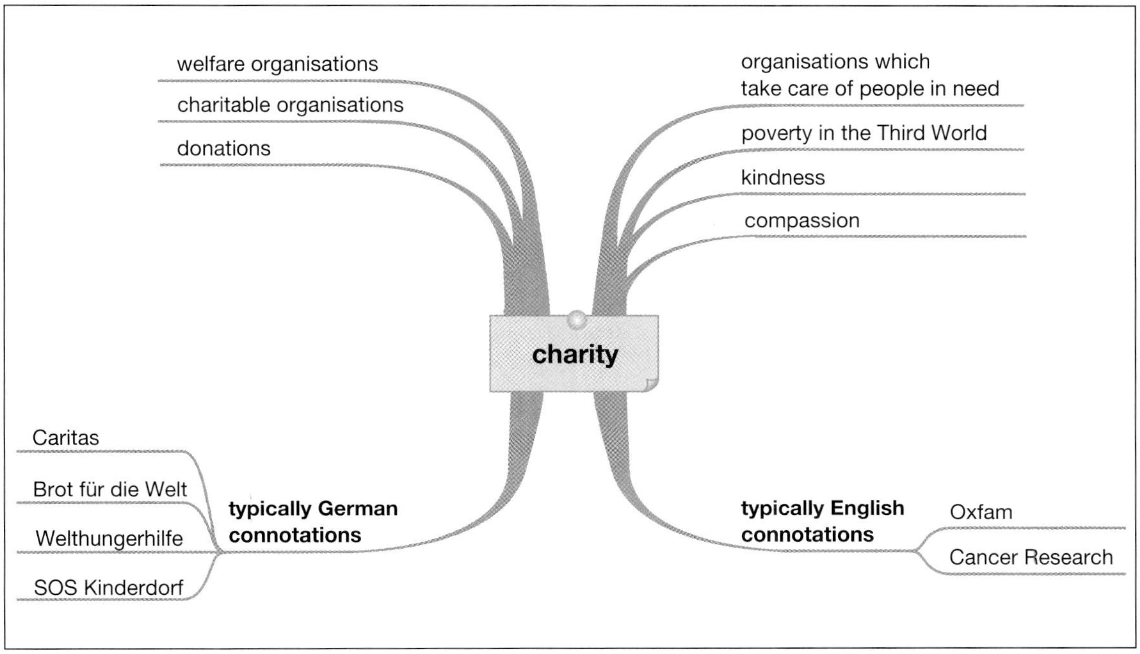

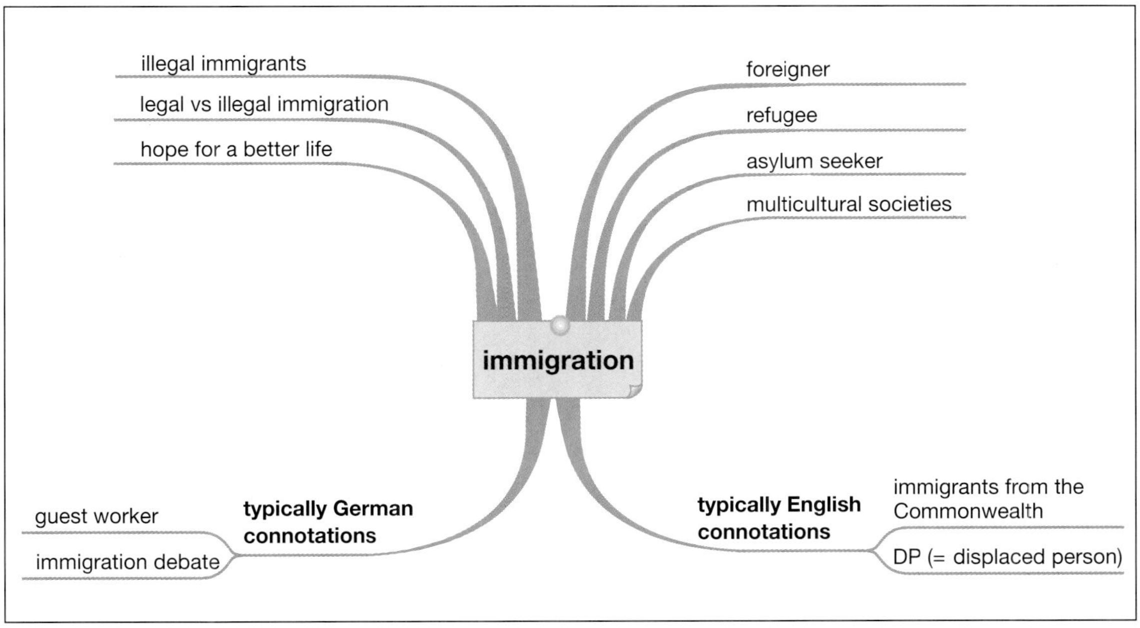

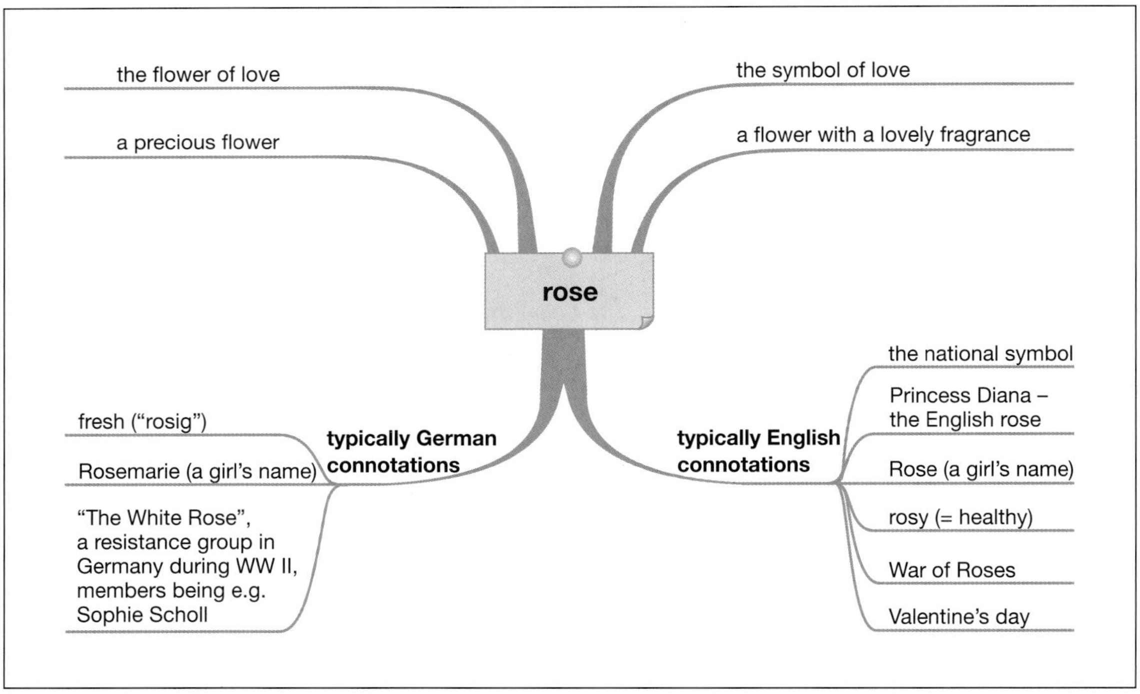

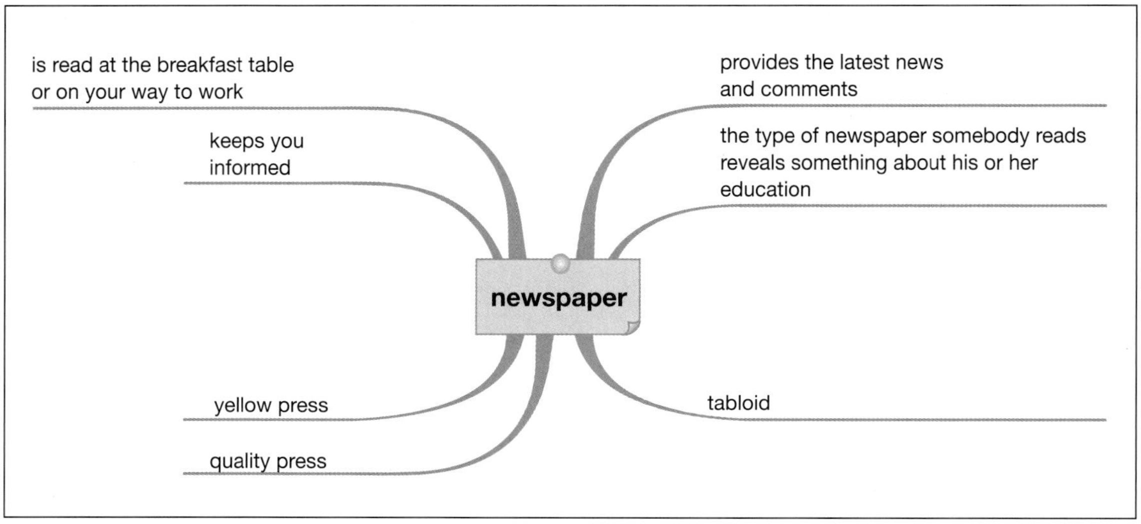

p. 17 ■ Classify the words of the following sentence under the different word classes.

Nowadays blacks still experience a great number of social disadvantages which proves that the civil rights movement never achieved the equality it promised.

Nouns: blacks, number, disadvantages, rights, movement, equality

Pronouns: it, which

Verbs: experience, proves, achieved, promised

Adjectives: great, social, civil

Adverbs: nowadays, still, never

Prepositions: of

Conjunctions: that

Determiners: a, the, the

p. 19 ■ Identify and underline as many collocations as possible in the following text.

[…] It all began this time <u>last year</u>, when black students decided that they would begin sharing the shade offered by the tree with their white counterparts, some of whom <u>regarded</u> it <u>as</u> their exclusive preserve.

The next morning three nooses were hanging from the boughs, an image intended to <u>remind</u> blacks <u>of</u> the lynchings once <u>inflicted on</u> their forebears. The white boys <u>found responsible</u> were given three days of <u>in-school suspension</u> after the education chiefs decided that their actions were nothing more than an <u>adolescent prank</u>.

But the incident <u>prompted</u> simmering <u>violence</u> between the two groups, which <u>came to a head</u> during the Thanksgiving holiday last November, when a fire at the school triggered a wave of fights and beatings.

<u>Lawyers representing</u> Mychal Bell, a <u>17-year-old</u> black student, <u>appealed</u> yesterday <u>to courts</u> to <u>set aside</u> his conviction by an <u>all-white jury</u> over an incident in which a white boy was <u>knocked unconscious</u>. Another five black teenagers were <u>charged with attempted murder</u> relating to the same incident. […]

<u>Civil rights leaders</u> are incensed by the apparent <u>double standards</u>, and are planning a march through the town <u>in support of</u> the "Jena Six" on September 20, when Bell is due to be sentenced. They say that white youths involved in the same <u>cycle of violence</u> faced significantly lesser charges or <u>have been released on probation</u>. […]

Tom Baldwin, The Times, 18.9.2007, p. 37

p. 20 ■ Match the right words to form collocations and form sentences with the collocations you have found.

to have a meeting	to gain experiences
to earn a living	to go on a trip
to break the news	to win a match
to take a long time	to get the flu
to make a mistake	to turn a page

- The students' representatives **have a meeting** in the common room next Tuesday at 4 pm.
- It's hard **to earn** a decent **living** when you are unemployed.
- The prime minister's resignation is today's **breaking news**.
- It **took** me **a long time** to find out your new address.
- He **made** a lot of **mistakes** that could have been avoided in his last class test.
- Spending a year in the U.S. I **gained** a lot of eye-opening **experiences**.
- We have decided **to go on a trip** to Australia after having passed our A-levels.
- Having **won** the last tennis **match** she is champion of her league.
- He got **the flu** when he went on holiday.
- Let's do some grammar exercises. Please **turn to page** 44.

p. 20 ■ Draw a collocation map for the keyword "opinion".

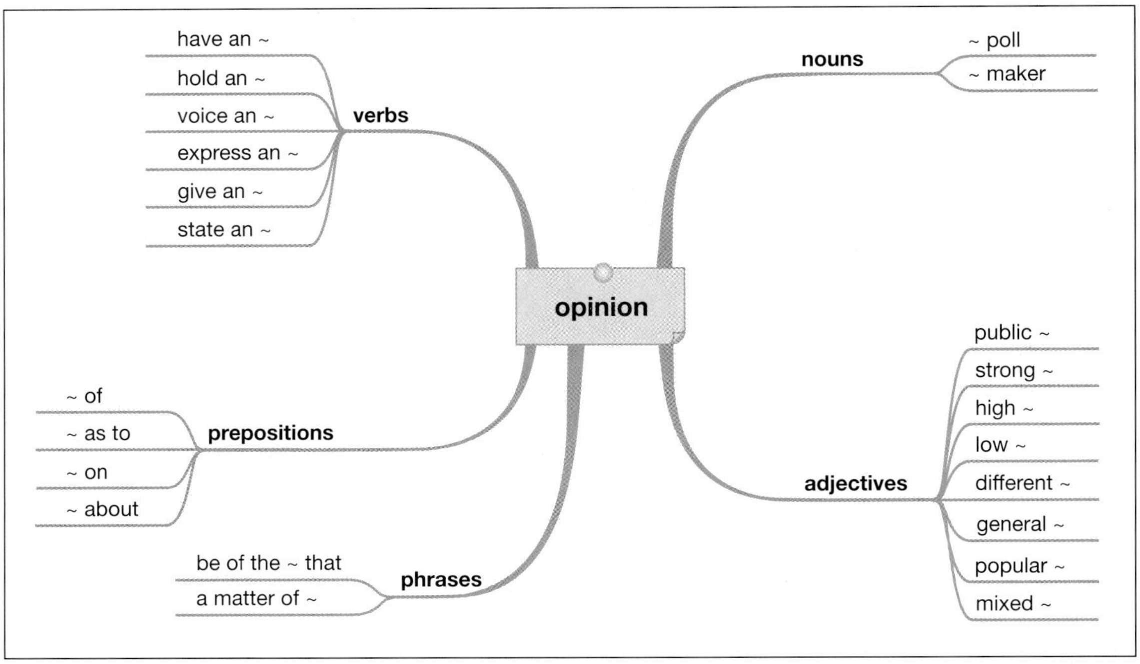

p. 21 ■ Have a look at the following sentences taken from two different letters of complaint, one to a friend and one to a mail-order bookshop. Which sentences are part of the letter to the mail-order bookshop and which sentences are part of the letter to a friend?

Letter to a friend

Hi Mary,

I'm just writing to tell you that I feel rather annoyed.

I asked you to send me some books I desperately needed for my exams 4 weeks ago.

Next time I ask you for something, please send it to me straight away, OK?

One of the books has had it. So I expect you to buy a new one.

What's more, I couldn't get hold of you on the phone.

I hope you are ok.

Take care, …

Letter to a mail-order bookshop

Dear Sir or Madam,

I am writing to express my dissatisfaction with your mail-order service.

I was very annoyed at having to wait 4 weeks for the books I had ordered.

What made matters worse was that when they eventually arrived one of the books was damaged in the post.

I expect you to replace the damaged books as soon as possible.

On top of all this, I couldn't reach anybody on your hotline.

I expect better service from a company of your reputation.

I look forward to hearing from you very soon.

Yours faithfully, …

How to find out the meaning of a word

p. 25 ■ Which German words do the following English words resemble?

English	German
minute	**Minute**
cathedral	**Kathedrale**
hand	**Hand**
fish	**Fisch**
shoe	**Schuh**
brown	**braun**
to begin	**beginnen**
disaster	**Desaster**
deficiency	**Defizit**

p. 26 ■ Find other words that resemble German or French words or words from other languages.

Examples:

- to accept (dt. akzeptieren, frz. accepter)
- accident (frz. l'accident, m.)
- butter (dt. die Butter)
- career (dt. die Karriere, frz. la carrière)
- to drink (dt. trinken)
- enormous (dt. enorm, frz. énorme)
- fortune (dt. Fortuna, frz. la fortune)
- frank (frz. franc/franche)
- to halt (dt. halten)
- list (dt. die Liste, frz. la liste)
- message (frz. le message)
- name (dt. der Name, frz. le nom)
- page (frz. la page)
- to reconcile (frz. réconcilier)
- season (dt. die Saison, frz. la saison)
- text (dt. der Text, frz. le texte)

p. 27 ■ Translate the following sentences. Beware of false friends.

1. Was ist deine Meinung? – **What's your opinion?**
2. Sie engagiert sich sehr für den Umweltschutz. – **She is committed to the protection of the environment.**
3. Was ist das Thema der heutigen Stunde? – **What is the topic of today's lesson?**
4. Susan hat sich zu einer selbstbewussten Frau entwickelt. – **Susan has developed into a self-confident woman.**
5. Steven ist frustriert, da er seine Idee nicht realisieren kann. – **Steven is frustrated because he cannot put his idea into practice.**
6. In Immobilien zu investieren, ist nicht mehr rentabel. – **To invest in property is not profitable anymore.**
7. Könnte ich dich eventuell am Wochenende sehen? – **Could I possibly come to see you at the weekend?**
8. Tom wird in der Schule gemobbt. – **Tom is bullied at school.**

p. 30 ■ Divide the following words up into their components.

	Prefix	Stem	Suffix
disadvantage	**dis**	**advant**	**age**
to rewind	**re**	**wind**	
to simplify		**simpli**	**fy**
meaningless		**meaning**	**less**
beautiful		**beauti**	**ful**
unbelievable	**un**	**believ**	**able**
indestructible	**in**	**destruct**	**ible**
unhappiness	**un**	**happi**	**ness**

p. 31 ■ Form new words by adding a prefix or a suffix and explain the new meaning of the word.

1. **im**possible – not possible
2. curios**ity** – the fact that somebody is curious to know something
3. treat**ment** – the action or result of treating somebody
4. decis**ion** – the action or result of deciding something
5. environment**al** – concerning the environment
6. beauti**ful** – full of beauty
7. **ir**responsible – not responsible
8. child**less** – without children

■ Form as many words as you can from the following prefixes, stems and suffixes.

Examples: interdisciplinary, international, reject, reread, report, reporter, recount, review, refer, reform, reformer, reformation, repaint, consider, considerable, consideration, conform, conformation, export, exporter, exportation, preview, prefer, preferable, preference, coexist, coexistence, instruct, instruction, infer, inference, disagree, disagreement, disagreeable, discount, discounter, deport, deportment, defer, deference, deferment, deform, deformation, unhappy, unhappiness

p. 32 ■ Find compounds made up of two nouns by matching words from the boxes below.

armchair	homework
bedtime	keyhole
brainstorm	lighthouse
copyright	molehill
daylight	newsletter
eyewitness	raincoat
footpath	nutshell

■ Find compounds made up of different kinds of words (e.g. nouns, verbs, prepositions) by matching words from the boxes below.

sunburn	lifelong
background	lovesick
counterattack	moonshine
downhill	shortsighted
ghostwriter	underdeveloped

p. 33 ■ Find more international words.

Examples:

anarchy	medium
balance	nomination
bureaucracy	phenomenon
chocolate	philosophy
criminality	protest
examination	revolution
generalization	sabotage
isolation	terrorist

p. 34 ■ Read the following sentences. The words in italics are nonsense words. With the help of the context, i.e. the words that come before and after nonsense words, try to work out their meaning.

❶ I was so **thirsty** that I drank a whole bottle of water.

❷ The sun is **shining**. Let's go out for a walk.

❸ As I didn't work hard enough I **failed** all my exams.

❹ **People** from all over the world come to see this stunning exhibition of 20th century art.

❺ Can you pass me the **newspaper**. I haven't read today's news yet.

❻ When we arrived at the airport we were informed that our **flight** had been cancelled.

How to memorize words

p. 43 ■ Find out about the meaning of the following words and involve as many senses as possible when memorizing them.

- to embrace – to put your arms around somebody in a kind way
- gentle – kind
- hedgehog – an animal with a lot of sharp needle-like spines
- mayhem – chaos
- fairground – an open space with stalls and amusements for entertainment and fun

p. 44 ■ Find words (nouns, verbs, adjectives) belonging to the same word family.

to die: death – death penalty – death row – death sentence – death bed – deathly – deathless – dead – deadness – deadly – to deaden – deadline – dead end

to disturb: disturbance – disturbed – disturbing

satisfaction: to satisfy – satisfactory – satisfactorily – satisfied – satisfying – satisfyingly – dissatisfaction – dissatisfied

aim: aim – aimlessly – aimlessness

p. 45 ■ Find synonyms and antonyms for the following words.

	Synonyms	Antonyms
to deteriorate	to worsen, to degenerate	to improve
exciting	thrilling, exhilarating	boring
to loathe	to hate, to detest	to love
miserable	unhappy, sad, depressed	happy, cheerful
illegal	forbidden, unlawful	legal, lawful
disdain	contempt, disgust	respect
furious	enraged, angry	calm
heat	warmth	cold
to pursue	to follow / to go after	to avoid
bias	prejudice	impartiality
important	significant	trivial

p. 47 ■ Organise the following words and expressions in word rows.

❶ obese – fat – chubby – slim – thin – skinny – bony

❷ to adore – to love – to like – to dislike – to hate – to loathe

❸ to book a room – to arrive at the hotel – to register at the reception – to enjoy your holiday – to pay the bill – to check-out – to return home

❹ to go to the station – to buy a ticket – to go to the platform – to get on the train – to find a seat – to store the luggage – to get off the train

■ Find words and expressions to create word rows starting as follows:

– tiny – small – medium – tall – huge

– birth – childhood – school – further or higher education – job career – family – retirement – death

– to study a recipe for a cake – to buy ingredients – to prepare necessary kitchen equipment – to preheat the oven – to mix ingredients – to pour into prepared pan – to bake – to allow to cool – to eat

p. 48 ■ Find hyponyms for the words "furniture" and "fruit".

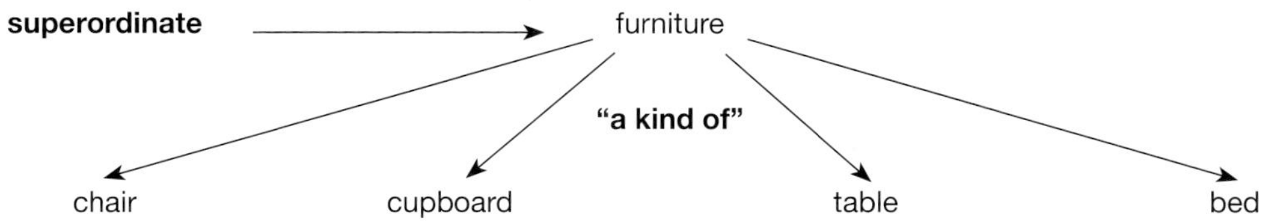

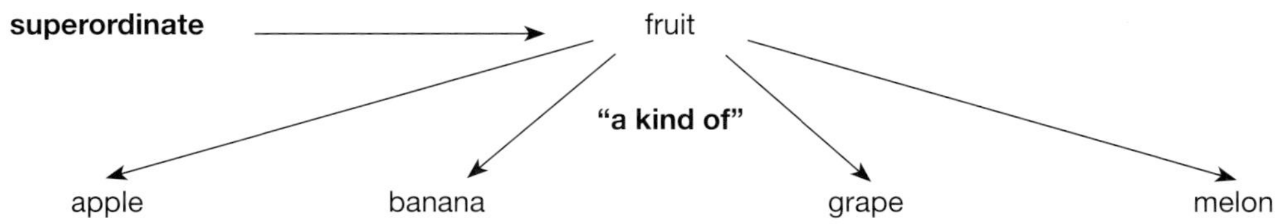

■ Find meronyms for the words "school" and "house".

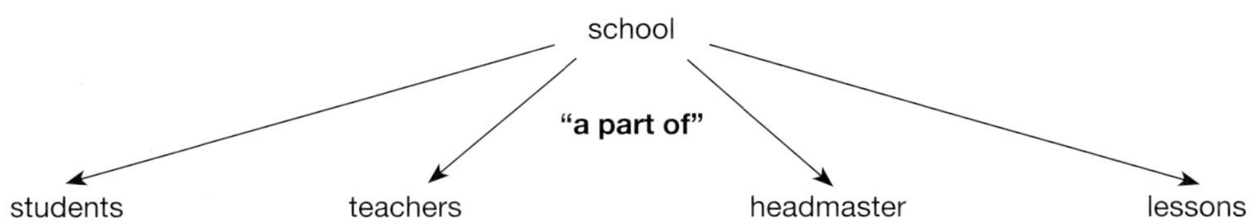

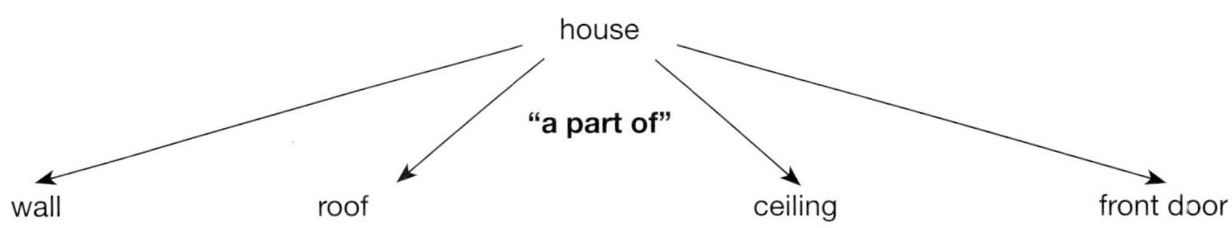

p. 53 ■ Match the following phrasal verbs with their synonym.

- to get back – to return
- to let down – to be disappointed
- to come round – to recover consciousness
- to turn up – to arrive
- to break down – to stop working
- to run out of – to come to an end
- to look into – to investigate
- to see someone off – to accompany someone about to set off on a journey

■ Identify and underline the phrasal verbs in the following sentences and explain their meaning.

1. We are planning to **do up** (to decorate) our living-room next autumn.
2. Can you **make out** (to see) the woman standing next to the church?
3. We've got enough room to **put** you **up** (to let sb stay) for the weekend.
4. You'll have to **do without** (to live without) your hat. I forgot it at home.
5. What do you **make of** (to think of) our new English teacher?
6. Tom always **gets away** (to be not punished) with his lies.
7. They were born in India, but they were **brought up** (to raise) in the U.S.

8 The airline's superb service **made up for** (to compensate for) all the inconveniences caused by the delay of our flight.

9 Susan always **comes up** (to have/to produce) with good ideas.

10 We'll have to **take on** (to employ) more staff to be able to finish the project in time.

11 The theatre is **putting on** (to perform) *Macbeth* next year.

12 Our children really **get on** (to like each other) well.

13 She **went on** (to continue) doing sports till her eighties.

14 He **took to** (to like) her at first sight.

15 I'm not **putting up with** (to accept) your bad mood anymore.

p. 54 ■ Match the following idioms with the corresponding expression.

- He's fallen **head over heels** in love with her. = *completely and thoughtlessly*
- When she left she **broke my heart**. = *to cause despair to another person*
- It's raining. That's why she has **got the blues** today. = *to be miserable*
- Climbing up that tree is not very difficult. Why not **have a go**? = *to try*
- We didn't book a flight in advance. We thought we'd just go to the airport and **take pot luck**. = *to leave things to chance*
- She hasn't eaten much lately. She is all **skin and bones**. = *very underweight*
- It's late. I think we should **make a move**. = *to go/leave*
- I really regret what I have done. I will have to **right a wrong**. = *to correct an unfair situation*
- She seems to have a good job. She is **coining money**. = *to earn a lot of money quickly and easily*
- Stop bothering me. You are **a pain in the neck**. = *a nuisance/a difficult person*
- **To put it in a nutshell**, this discussion is a waste of time. = *to say it in a few words*
- Coming face to face with the bear, I felt **scared stiff**. = *to be very scared*

p. 55 ■ Match the following proverbs with the corresponding paraphrases.

- **Don't count your chickens before they're hatched**. = *Don't make plans for the future too early*.
- **Barking dogs seldom bite**. = *Those who loudly threat to do something rarely do so*.
- **Any time means no time**. = *If something is not planned it will never take place*.
- **Too many cooks spoil the broth**. = *Things will go wrong if too many people interfere*.
- **Call a spade a spade**. = *Someone speaks frankly and directly*.
- **A friend in need is a good friend indeed**. = *A friend who helps when you are in trouble is a true friend*.
- **Between the devil and the deep blue sea**. = *You have to choose between two equally bad alternatives*.
- **There is no smoke without fire**. = *Rumours are usually based on some truth*.

p. 56 ■ Imagine situations in which you would use the social formulae mentioned above.

You use ...

– How are you? I'm fine.	... when you meet somebody you know.
– What's up? What's new?	... when you ask somebody for the latest news.
– I'd better get going.	... when you are about to leave.
– See you later./Have a nice day.	... when you leave somebody.
– Nice to meet you./Pleased to meet you.	... when you meet somebody for the first time.
– Let's get together some time.	... when you arrange to meet somebody.
– Sit down and make yourself at home.	... when you welcome somebody at home.
– Please help yourself.	... when you let somebody choose and take what he/she wants to eat.

– Thank you. You're welcome. ... when you thank somebody for something.
– I'd like you to meet ... ... when you want to introduce somebody to somebody.

p. 59 ■ Create an acrostic from the following word: GENETIC ENGINEERING. Try to find words which have to do with the topic "genetic engineering". Write a short text integrating all the words you have found.

Genetic
Engineering
Necessary
Embryo
Transplant
Inherit
Cloning

Ethical
Natural
Gene
In vitro fertilization
Normal
Experiment
Extinct
Research
Invention
Need
GM food

Cloning and **GM food** require **genetic engineering** whereas for **in vitro fertilization** it is **necessary** to **transplant** an **embryo**. Of course, the **ethical** question is what is **normal** and **natural** in these **experiments**. Whatever happens, the **genes** we **inherit** won't become **extinct** unless **research** and new **inventions** force the scientists to meet modern **need**.

p. 60 ■ Using the keyword method memorize the following words: to apply for a job. Draw a picture.

How to keep records of words

p. 74 ■ Here is a list of English words which have to do with "the media". Organise them in a systematic word list. Add more words and expressions connected to the topic.

English	German	Example sentences	Useful tips
to communicate with sb	mit jdm kommunizieren		to communicate by e-mail communication
mass media	Massenmedien		dangers of mass media
to inform about	informieren		sources of information
to report on sth.	berichten über	She made an excellent ~ on the school's different clubs.	a full / detailed report on sth
to entertain	unterhalten	A lot of TV shows are supposed to ~ people.	entertaining entertainment ↔ to bore
sensational	aufsehenerregend		= fantastic/thrilling sensationalism

influence on	Einfluss		to have/exert a strong influence on sb to influence sb influential
to become addicted to	abhängig werden	A lot of young people ~ computer games.	addiction
to censor sth	etw. zensieren		censor censorship
controversial	umstritten	The report is about a highly ~ topic, the death penalty.	controversy
to protect consumers	Verbraucher schützen		
means of communication	Kommunikationsmittel	Modern ~ enable people all around the world to communicate.	
mobile phone	Handy	Nowadays, a lot of people cannot live without their ~ anymore.	False friend! engl. handy – dt. handlich, praktisch
a local call	ein lokaler Anruf		↔ a long-distance call an urgent call
phonecard	Telefonkarte		
engaged	besetzt	I can't get through to her. Her phone has been ~ for the last 30 minutes.	= busy the engaged tone
letter	Brief		to post/to send/ to receive a letter/ a postcard/a parcel
fax machine	Faxgerät		
radio	Radio		to listen to the radio
listener	Zuhörer		
to transmit	übertragen		transmission
to tune	einstellen	He ~ his radio.	
TV	Fernsehen		to watch TV
to broadcast	senden	The interview with the Queen will be ~ live tomorrow.	
viewer	Zuschauer		
picture	Bild		in the picture
feature	Fernsehbeitrag		

news	Nachrichten	What's in the ~ today?	to break the news
weather forecast	Wettervorhersage	The ~ said it would be fine all day.	
soap opera	Seifenoper		
documentary	Dokumentarfilm	Have you seen the latest ~ on global warming?	
press	Presse		
publication	Veröffentlichung		to publish a book
readership	Leserschaft	Every newspaper attracts its own particular ~.	
newspaper	Zeitung		quality newspaper popular newspaper
tabloid	Boulevardzeitung	"The Sun" is an English, the "Bild" is a German ~.	
news magazine	Nachrichtenmagazin		
caption	Überschrift/Bildunter-schrift		
headline	Überschrift	The ~ tries to attract the reader's attention.	the headlines to make headlines
photo	Foto		
editorial	Leitartikel		
current affairs	Tagesgeschehen		
to subscribe to	abonnieren	We ~ to the local news-paper.	subscription fee
the Internet	das Internet	More and more people do their shopping on the ~.	to surf the Internet
e-mail	E-Mail		to send an e-mail
to design a website	eine Webseite entwerfen	You do not need to be a computer expert to be able to ~.	
data processing	Datenverarbeitung		
data protection	Datenschutz		
advertisement	Werbung		to advertise
commercial	Werbefernsehen	People complain about too many ~ interrupting the programmes of private TV stations.	a TV/radio commercial

How to expand your vocabulary

p. 80

■ Read the following text about organic food. Highlight all the words and expressions that belong to the lexical field "Organic food". Organise them in a systematic way or with the help of a visualizing technique (➜ pp. 69 – 72). Add more words and expressions connected to the topic. If you want you can use a dictionary.

Organic food helps revive fortunes of Europe's farmers

The **organic revolution** is sweeping across Europe, with the area of land dedicated to **environmentally-friendly, pesticide-free food production** more than doubling in the last decade.
Organic farming now accounts for more than 4 per cent of **agricultural land** in the EU, more than double its 1998 share, according to a new report from its official statistics agency, Eurostat.
And **organic land** is likely to make greater inroads, as the **consumer appetite** shows no sign of slowing. "**Organic** almost certainly will continue to grow and we think it's a good thing," Michael Mann, an **EU agriculture spokesman** said.
The growth is partly being driven by Europe's **farmers**, who are being undercut by **produce** imported from countries such as Brazil. For many farmers, **organic foods** are becoming a key way to **reinvent their failing farms**. [...]
Conscious of this **ballooning market**, **agriculture ministers** from the 27 member states **agreed** this week **on a compulsory logo**, to be introduced from 2009, designed to reassure **consumers** that they are getting the genuine article.
The logo guarantees that at least 95 per cent of ingredients are completely **free of chemicals** – and imports will be subject to the same rule. But it also permits up to 0.9 per cent from **genetically-modified organisms**, a level that has angered **green campaigners**.
"It is a total cop-out by the European Union – setting a level of 0.9 per cent could result in the creeping **GM contamination of organic food**," said Ben Ayliffe, of Greenpeace. "It should be 0.1 per cent."
"Go into any supermarket and they are bursting with **organic food**, while **GM foods** are conspicuous by their absence. That's because **consumers** don't want them!" he added.
In recent years, European **consumers** have shown themselves willing to pay more for **organic produce**, reflecting **an aversion to chemicals** and a **growing preference for natural farming techniques** over the **high-intensity production** that has been blamed for crises such as **BSE** and **foot-and-mouth disease**.
Recognising this fact, Brussels will now provide higher levels of **subsidy** for **organic farming** than that given to **non organic fruit and vegetables**.
The UK has been **a leader in organic farming**. In 2005, more than 600,000 hectares of the country's **farmland were cultivated organically**, putting it ahead of France, a country more than twice its size. Yet only 3.8 per cent of UK farmland was **devoted to organic production**, compared with 11 per cent in Austria. The Alpine nation has a reputation as a strong **opponent of intensive and bio-tech farming**, recently refusing to **follow an EU ruling** allowing a type of **genetically-modified maize** made by Monsanto.
While the Eurostat report primarily compared the 15 nations that joined the EU before 2004, it also pointed out that some of the biggest **organic farms** now are to be found in newcomers Slovakia and Czech Republic.

Adam Mitchell and Rachel Shields, The Independent, 14.6.2007, p. 27

Association network "Organic food"

organic farming

organic revolution

a ballooning market

organic farms

organic land

to be devoted to organic production

environmentally-friendly

pesticide-free food production

free of chemicals

to be cultivated organically

organic produce

GM contamination of organic food

growing pressure from low-cost producers

to increase profit margins

to reinvent failing farms

to become a leader in organic farming

intensive farming

agricultural land

farmland

to cultivate crops

crop cultivation

to yield crops

at the expense of the environment

to use fertilizers and pesticides

organic food

high-intensity production

non organic fruit and vegetables

genetically-modified organisms

GM foods

genetically-modified maize

diseases

BSE

foot-and-mouth disease

players

consumers

consumer appetite

an aversion to chemicals

growing preference for natural farming techniques

farmers

international politics

EU agriculture spokesman

agriculture ministers

to provide subsidies

to follow an EU ruling

to agree on a compulsory logo

NGOs

green campaigners

opponents of intensive and biotech farming

How to work with a dictionary

p. 88 ■ Study the following word entry. What information is provided?

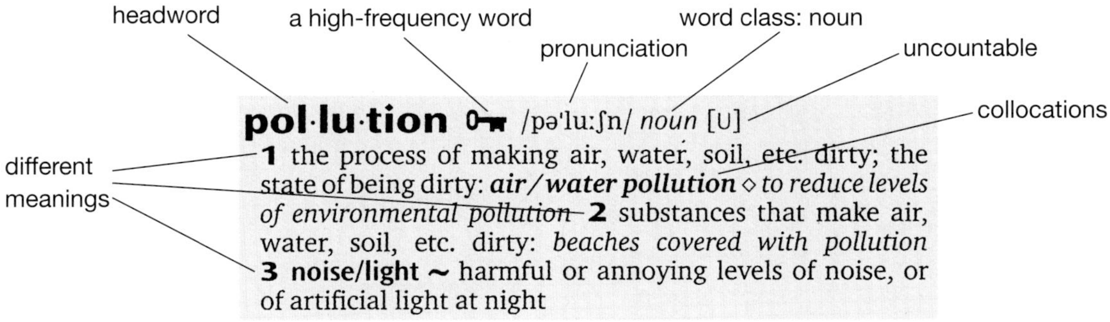

pol·lu·tion /pəˈluːʃn/ *noun* [U] **1** the process of making air, water, soil, etc. dirty; the state of being dirty: ***air/water pollution*** ◇ *to reduce levels of environmental pollution* **2** substances that make air, water, soil, etc. dirty: *beaches covered with pollution* **3 noise/light ~** harmful or annoying levels of noise, or of artificial light at night

A. S. Hornby. Oxford Advenced Learner's Dictionary of Current English. Oxford, Oxford University Press, 2005

p. 89 Use your dictionary to answer the following questions.

■ Rank the following words in terms of frequency.

1. sick – ill – unwell
2. specific – particular – peculiar

■ Cross the odd one out as far as pronunciation is concerned.

1. ~~albeit~~ – conceit – deceit
2. soar – saw – ~~sue~~
3. daughter – ~~laughter~~ – slaughter
4. swallow – blow – ~~sow~~

■ Choose the correct pronunciation.

1. [waʊnd]
2. [bəʊ]
3. [maɪˈnjuːt]

p. 90 ■ Which word classes do the following words belong to?

1. hollow – adjective, noun, verb
2. fine – adjective, adverb, verb, noun

■ Complete the table with the correct forms.

Verb	Noun	Adjective	Adverb
to protect	protection	protected/protective	protectively
to beautify	beauty	beautiful	beautifully
to rely	reliability/reliance	reliable/reliant	reliably
to care	care	careful	carefully

■ Find out what the abbreviations stand for.

1. VIP – very important person
2. YMCA – Young Men's Christian Association
3. BBC – British Broadcasting Corporation
4. MP – Member of Parliament

■ Decide which words fit best into the following sentences:

1. Your **duties** will include looking after the children.
2. The organisation is fighting against child **labour**.
3. School leavers are finding it more and more difficult to find **employment**.
4. This is a difficult **task**. I wonder if I can get it done today.
5. Every morning I go to **work** at 8 o'clock.
6. She had a life full of hardship and **toil**.
7. He lost his **job** last month. Now he is unemployed.

■ Decide which word fits in which sentence.

1. We arrived at our **destination** safe and sound.
   It was his **destiny** to die young.
2. You have to ask the teacher for **permission**.
   You're not allowed to park here without a special **permit**.
3. She knows exactly what she wants. She is a **self-confident** woman.
   He doesn't like speaking in front of many people. He is very **self-conscious**.
4. I'm **convinced** he is not guilty.
   He was **convicted** of murder.

p. 91 ■ Find the opposites (antonyms) of the following words.

1. important – unimportant
2. adequate – inadequate
3. legible – illegible
4. smoker – non-smoker

■ Match the following words.

- odds and ends
- law and order
- sooner or later
- give and take
- out and about
- back and forth

■ Complete the following idiomatic expressions.

1. Susan is head and **shoulders** above the rest of the girls.
2. She has got a **chip** on her shoulder.
3. She is a bit of an odd-**ball**.
4. I was scared **stiff**.

■ Find out which of the following verbs take the -ing-form and which take the to-infinitive.

1. (to) consider + **-ing**
2. (to) admit + **-ing**
3. (to) promise + **to-infinitive**
4. (to) mind + **-ing**

■ Fill in the correct prepositions in the following sentences.

1. She had difficulties **in** finding her way home.
2. I'm tired **of** waiting any longer.
3. I don't see any possibility **of** coming to the party tonight.
4. This is a nice example **of** Greek history.

p. 92 ■ Match the following phrasal verbs with the appropriate meaning.

– I must be **seeing** things.	have hallucinations
– I must **see to** my homework.	deal with
– They've gone to **see** Jane **off** at the station.	accompany sb who is about to set off on a journey
– It's difficult to **see through** his behaviour.	not deceived by

■ Find the plurals of the following nouns.

1. crisis – crises
2. supply – supplies
3. information – information/pieces of information
4. phenomenon – phenomena

■ Find out the forms of the past tense and the past participle of the following verbs.

Infinitive	Past tense	Past participle
to light	lit/lighted	lit/lighted
to hit	hit	hit
to kneel	knelt/kneeled	knelt/kneeled
to dig	dug	dug

■ What are the British equivalents of the following American forms?

1. sidewalk – pavement
2. restroom – toilet
3. vacation – holiday
4. truck – lorry

How to use your words

p. 93 ■ How many words are there in the word "Commonwealth"?

common, comma, come, cot, oat, owe, own, name, wet, wealth, whale, what, wheat, won, woman, ale, alone, lame, lot, low, law, lawn, home, hot, halt, heal, hem, helm, how, howl, ham, hole, tan, ten, tame, the, then, than, tow, towel, toe, mow, mole, moth, man, men, moon, mean, …

p. 94 ■ Write an acrostic with the word DISCRIMINATION and write a short text which contains all the words you have found.

Disdainful
Immigrant
Shameful
Control
Recommendation
Invite
Myth
Interracial
News
Attitude
Trade
Influence
Occasion
Non-profit

The way **immigrants** are treated on **occasions** is **disdainful** and **shameful**. It would be a good idea to **invite** them into your home to get rid off **interracial** prejudices.
A **recommendation** to exercise some kind of **control** on the **news**, which **influences** our **attitudes**, would be advisable.
Very often the immigrants have to work in a **trade** which for them is almost on a **non-profit** basis, thus doing away with the **myth** that they are only living off the state.

p. 97 ■ Look out for 10 words in the following word search puzzle containing words on the topic "Multicultural Britain".

G	R	A	G	H	J	B	J	K	T	I	**C**	A	Q	R	H	G	J	K	G
P	A	**I**	**M**	**M**	**I**	**G**	**R**	**A**	**T**	**I**	**O**	**N**	H	J	K	T	K	Z	D
F	**R**	A	D	H	B	M	D	K	T	R	**M**	E	I	K	R	J	K	H	K
C	H	**E**	E	Y	H	V	R	F	H	V	**M**	S	Y	E	I	A	**N**	**N**	S
H	A	A	**J**	I	E	G	A	S	Z	O	**O**	Z	G	I	L	J	**O**	D	N
I	G	E	M	**U**	G	H	Q	E	R	T	**N**	S	A	F	O	**I**	**I**	C	F
L	V	G	**E**	W	**D**	G	J	K	B	N	**W**	C	R	I	**T**	S	**T**	A	E
N	M	B	**E**	E	D	**I**	F	G	H	Z	**E**	V	N	**A**	H	I	**U**	N	M
A	K	I	**G**	W	D	F	**C**	A	F	E	**A**	L	**I**	N	I	O	**C**	M	K
W	P	U	**U**	W	V	N	I	**E**	B	H	**L**	**R**	E	N	M	J	**E**	G	U
E	**I**	**N**	**F**	**L**	**U**	**X**	W	N	M	H	**T**	Z	I	O	K	P	**S**	M	L
F	S	A	**E**	W	R	G	U	I	O	**A**	**H**	A	H	S	N	H	**R**	T	H
JV	R	V	**R**	Y	V	F	W	B	**P**	E	**C**	H	J	F	R	S	**E**	E	O
H	A	N	S	W	D	E	G	**E**	G	J	**I**	T	E	V	J	N	**P**	Y	D
J	H	X	G	J	T	B	**R**	T	J	E	**T**	O	H	Z	T	D	E	G	J
K	V	M	E	E	K	Z	S	H	**T**	**C**	**I**	**R**	**T**	**S**	**E**	**R**	T	E	K
L	J	L	G	G	J	H	T	A	W	O	**Z**	A	G	Q	R	I	G	S	G
T		O	A	**A**	**S**	**Y**	**L**	**U**	**M**	**S**	**E**	**E**	**K**	**E**	**R**	G	P	A	R
I	M	D	J	N	I	L	G	U	K	S	**N**	B	H	E	G	J	Z	H	E
E	**T**	**H**	**N**	**I**	**C**	**D**	**I**	**V**	**E**	**R**	**S**	**I**	**T**	**Y**	M	M	O	J	W

p. 100 ■ Try to fill in the gaps in the following text on migration to and from Great Britain.

A day in the life of a shifting population: the 2,500 migrants who come in and out

Up to 500 Britons a day are acting on their dreams of upping sticks and **moving** to a new home. **Record** numbers **emigrated** from the UK last year, with Australia, Spain and France topping the list of preferred destinations.
The scale of the exodus emerged yesterday as government **figures** painted a dramatic picture of "departure lounge Britain". Some 1,500 **immigrants** arrived in the UK every day in 2005, with people from Poland leading the **influx**, while 1,000 left the country.
Half of them were UK **nationals** opting for a life **abroad**, mainly attracted by work **opportunities**, a lower cost of **living** and the prospect of retirement in warmer climates. One in five **headed** for Australia, where many Britons already have relatives, research by the Office for National Statistics showed. Large numbers also **emigrated** to Spain, where a large expatriate retirement community lives, and France, which has surged in popularity with Britons over the past decade.
Thousands also chose the United States, which is recovering in popularity since the September 11 terrorist attacks, and New Zealand.
Of the other nationalities that left Britain last year, 56,000 were from the EU; 40,000 from "old **Commonwealth**" countries such as Australia, New Zealand and South Africa; 24,000 from "new Commonwealth" **nations** and 62,000 from other countries.
The UK, in common with much of the Western world, has **experienced** high levels both of **immigration** and emigration for a decade. The numbers settling in this country for at least 12 months fell slightly last year to 565,000, with poles representing the single largest group of **incomers**. Over the same period, 00 people **left the country** – half of them foreign nationals and half of them Britons emigrating abroad. […]
In 2005, 80,000 east Europeans settled in Britain, mainly from Poland. This was the first full year of the European Union membership of eight former Soviet-bloc countries. At the same time, 15,000 east Europeans **returned** home, suggesting that the numbers from those countries in Britain **increased** by 65,000 over the year.
The **figures** also confirm that the vast majority of east European workers who come to the UK […] stay in the country for less than a year.
High numbers of immigrants came from south Asia last year, including India, Pakistan and Bangladesh, as well as the "old Commonwealth" countries. And 15,000 Americans **settled** in Britain – mainly for work – while significant numbers of Spaniards and Germans also **made the move**.
The net inflow of **asylum seekers** fell to 11,000 from a record high of 81,000 five years earlier. It is the lowest figure for more than a decade.

Nigel Morris, The Independent, 3.11.2006, p. 5

How to cope with word gaps

p. 104 ■ Find a way of explaining the following words.

1. Bankfiliale = a company that provides financial services (paraphrase)
2. Humbug = nonsense, rubbish (synonyms)
3. Nikolaus = resembles Father Christmas, but whereas Father Christmas comes on the 24th December and brings a lot of Christmas presents, "Nikolaus" comes on the 6th December and puts sweets into the children's boots or stockings while they are sleeping (paraphrase)
4. Gelatine = you need it to make jelly bears (example)